"Some leaders talk about the ministry of revitalization without ever doing the work. That's not the case with Pastor Rob Beckett; he writes from the overflow of his experience. This book is a well-thought-out guide to renewing the vision of the local church. It includes practical steps for reaching the community and leading people to faith in Christ. Rob takes his readers on a step-by-step journey that reveals how revitalization is possible in any context. I highly recommend *Fanning the Revitalization Flame*"

-Dr. Brian L. Powell
District Superintendent
Kentucky District Church of the Nazarene

Rob's writing is grounded by the laboratory of raw and messy local church life and community outreach in rural communities. Rob's longevity in his pastoral assignments along with his creative and relentless efforts to meet the needs of his neighbors make him someone worthy of our attention.

-Dr. Scott Sherwood
President, Nazarene Bible College

"Fanning the Revitalization Flame" is a powerful book – it really impacted my heart as I read through the pages. This is a much-needed resource for our churches today! Rob has not only carefully laid out the crisis in many of our churches today but has also provided glorious hope for our restoration and destiny. This isn't a book filled with empty rhetoric - it is a book based on experience and wisdom fueled by a fiery passion for revival. The practical application moves this book from another "good idea" for church growth to real steps on the road to spiritual revitalization! God's way and for His glory!

-Rhonda Mathisen (Hughey)
Author, *Desperate for His Presence*

This is a must-read book for any pastor or church leader who desires to see the church experience renewal and revitalization!

Most of us know our churches need revitalization but struggle with the practical steps to launch the journey. Rev. Robert Beckett has a proven track record of bringing revitalization to the church, and as he writes, it is as if he is responding to your thoughts and questions. So, what are you waiting for? Start reading and begin helping the church experience revitalization.

-Dr. Timothy Crump
District Superintendent
Southwest Indiana District Church of the Nazarene

What a pleasant surprise to have so much valuable information tucked into Pastor Rob Beckett's book *Fanning the Revitalization Flame*. Every rural (or even urban) church will find practical ideas to employ and see God do a new thing in their ministry. The book is comprehensive and completed by Pastor Rob's own experiences of revitalizing his own church. Even if you feel it's too late, absorb and apply this content and you too can bring new life to your ministry.

-Rev. Elaine Briefman
Shepherd, author, speaker, and owner
Fishing4Truth Ministry Success

Revitalization - more than a word, but a practice. Pastor, leader, author, and friend Rob Beckett takes us through the process in this book. He presents the case for "new wineskins" and a fresh work of the Holy Spirit. Not only will your church be revitalized, but so will you.

-Rev. Jay Height
Executive Director
Shepherd Community

Rob Beckett beautifully weaves his own journey as a rural church pastor into the narrative of *Fanning the Revitalization Flame*. His is not the search for some newfangled approach or strategy. His call is for a return to the old paths. The reader will sense Rob's passion to show you the way up from despair and hopelessness to transformation and fruitfulness as a thriving community of faith, starting with a change of perception.

-Dr. David F. Nixon
Author, *It Only Takes a Spark*
District Superintendent Emeritus
South Florida District of the Church of the Nazarene

Rob has a way of looking at the church, the community, and people and seeing that God has so much more for each of them than most have come to believe. He will challenge you to do the same and, in the process, you will find yourself encouraged as a pastor of a small church that has great Kingdom potential.

-Heath Barth
Campus Pastor
Southeast Christian Church

Fanning
the
REVITALIZATION
FLAME

*Leading Your Church from Smoldering
Embers to Revival Fire*

Robert Beckett

WESTBOW
PRESS®
A DIVISION OF THOMAS NELSON
& ZONDERVAN

WestBow Press books may be ordered through booksellers or by contacting:

WestBow Press
A Division of Thomas Nelson & Zondervan
1663 Liberty Drive
Bloomington, IN 47403
www.westbowpress.com
844-714-3454

Unless otherwise indicated, all Scripture taken from the New King James Version®. Copyright © 1982 by Thomas Nelson. Used by permission. All rights reserved.

Scripture quotations marked (AMP) are taken from the Amplified Bible, Copyright © 1954, 1958, 1962, 1964, 1965, 1987 by The Lockman Foundation. Used by permission.

ISBN: 978-1-6642-8467-8 (sc)
ISBN: 978-1-6642-8468-5 (hc)
ISBN: 978-1-6642-8466-1 (e)

Library of Congress Control Number: 2022921646

Print information available on the last page.

WestBow Press rev. date: 12/06/2022

CONTENTS

DEDICATION

For my wife, Joanna, putting up with the good and the bad. She is willing to follow anywhere Jesus leads. Her heart is for serving others as Jesus wants. She put away a nice job, in which she had much vested time, so that she could work more closely to the ones who are in need, who are living lives of brokenness. She runs a center for homeless women and children, providing much needed resources and the face of Jesus to the ones she encounters day to day. You make the world a better place.

I want to give a special thanks to the ladies who help with adjusting my West Virginia-ese so that the book could be a little more readable. Thank you, Karen Meadows, Lois Merrell, Roberta Falkenstein Steutermann for the edits and spell checking, and also Jay Height for the encouragement and mentorship that you provide, which has been priceless.

To my Shepherdsville First Church family. This has been a journey that has seen many ups and downs, but it has been worth it all. I love each one of you. We have been able to see lives transformed and saved from the clutches of the enemy. This is only the beginning of the story because we still have a lot of work to do!

To my Papa Herman - although he died many years before I was ever called to preach, he has been a constant guide for me as a pastor. Watching him as I grew up on that front row with him setting the example of how a strong Christian man should be will never leave me. Papa, I sure loved listening to you preach God's Word with power and authority.

FOREWORD

The future of the church in the world today rests on the effectiveness of the small church. The small church seems to be a part of God's plan. At the end of our Lord's ministry, he had established a small band of believers: a small church. His Holy Spirit birthed the church by training 12 church planters. When the first church in Jerusalem became large, he dispersed it so that, in just a matter of decades, the church could have little outposts all across the known world. The small church seems to be central to God's ordained strategy for reaching the world. As Director of the Church of the Nazarene's work in the USA and Canada, I realize the key role small churches must have in our mission.

Today, the Church of the Nazarene is very similar to most movements of churches: the average size of our 5,000 churches is about 50 people. With so many small churches, it is more important than ever for them to have access to the resources to make the big impact God has in mind. Pastor Rob Beckett is the perfect person to provide these invaluable resources.

I know Pastor Rob Beckett as a friend; I know his heart. He loves small churches, their pastors and people. He has put his heart and soul into writing this book; this is a labor of love and gift to the church.

I also know Pastor Rob Beckett as a an intelligent, highly skilled pastor. He has the gifts and graces to pastor any sized church, yet he has intentionally chosen to shepherd the small church. Since he believes, as I do, that small churches are essential to God's holy purpose, he wants to be in the center of what God is doing.

This book will walk the reader through every step that is needed for the revitalization of the small church. Starting in prayer, moving to exegeting the community, mission vision, strategy, resourcing and doing the work. Following these steps, Pastor Beckett has moved his small church to make a transformative difference in lives in his community. The results are undeniable. The changed lives has changed every metric in his small church, including an income of $35,000 moving to over $100,000 in just a few years. Changed hearts change everything!

This book is a must read for every small church pastor, board member, and everyone who desires to make a holy positive impact on the community in which God has providentially placed them. Read these pages and you will begin to see how God intends to do great work in every community through 1000s of revitalized small churches.

I want to personally thank Rob Beckett for his love and labor to resource a sleeping giant - the small church - to arise and fulfill God's purpose to change the world.

-**Dr. Stan Reeder**
Director, USA/Canada Region
Church of the Nazarene

INTRODUCTION

smol·der

verb

To burn slowly with smoke but no flame

I grew up in a rural area of Cabell County, West Virginia. We lived just above the coalfields of southern West Virginia and in the foothills just west of the Appalachian Mountains. We lived in the part of the state known as the Tri-State area, West Virginia, Ohio, and Kentucky all right there together. My time there was from the early '60s through the early '90s.

I grew up in a time when we went to school and every morning the first things we would do when we started class that day was to pray the Lord's prayer and to stand up and put our hands on our hearts and say the pledge allegiance to America. We would also say grace over our food at lunchtime. On Sundays, everyone I knew went to church and Sunday School. There was never any question whether you did, it was just what everybody did. Also, I remember on Sunday stores closed so that they could observe Sunday rest.

One of my fondest memories and first memories of the church is my papa picking us up to take us to Sunday school every Sunday. It was a treat to be able to set alongside him on the front pew during the service. I may be biased, but my papa was a wonderful man of God. He showed us love, gentleness, caring, and everything that a good Christian man should show his grandsons. The church we attended was a small country church but exhibited faith and a love for God that showed to everyone in the community. Many times, as we had service people would have to stand up in the back because there were not enough seats. People came to every service and anticipated a move of God every time. And God did show up many, many times. It was a regular occurrence to see people going to the altar and praying and being released from the hold of sin, being saved, testifying, shouting, and praising God openly and freely.

In this small country church, it was normal to see people of the church gathering together to help a family or help an individual that was sick or out of work or needed some type of help, and the church would step in and help them as one body. They would go and visit people that were shut-ins or sick or not able to come to church. When somebody moved new into the community the leaders of the church would go and visit and welcome them and invite them to church.

We live in a completely different time now. It is not like it used to be. You would be hard-pressed to be able to find a church nowadays that exhibits the hand, feet, and heart of Christ like this anymore. Churches today are struggling just to keep their doors open and the lights on. Attendance has fallen off so drastically that many churches are closing every week all across America. Pastors and leaders are struggling just to be able to keep their church together and to keep their ministries from falling apart. Pastors are being discouraged and depressed and seem like they don't know which way to turn even within their own denominations. Many pastors are leaving the ministry one after another, it has been said that out of 10 students that come out of ministry training only two will get to retirement.

It is no longer a question of whether the Church in the West is struggling or not…it is a plain fact. Everywhere you turn it seems that you see struggling churches, struggling pastors, and struggling congregations. The fire has seemed to die out in the Western church today. The days when I grew up and the fire seemed to be strong in the church are no longer the case. Many times, there are barely even embers left in many congregations. What the church needs today is the fire of God to fall upon them, to ignite them again into a strong, vibrant, and effective church.

But the church and the people must want it first. God will not barge his way in the front doors of a church and make anyone do anything that they don't want to do. God is calling His church today to wake up and let the fire burn inside them again as it did once before when that church first started. God wants the Holy Spirit to be able to blow His breath on those smoldering embers of all congregations of all people all over America, to breathe on them, and for the fire to burn in their sanctuary and their community again.

It is my hope and my prayer that this book may be able to help in some way to encourage and ignite the fire in a congregation and/or pastor again so that they can be an effective and contributing neighbor in their neighborhood. A church should be the best neighbor that your neighborhood has. Many things are wrong today in the world and our churches, but may you be the first step for that change in your community and in your context. God wants to take your church and to let Him shine in and through it.

There are people all around us that need to hear and know of the good news that we must share and that is the gospel of Jesus Christ to everyone that does not have a personal intimate relationship with Him. It is our responsibility to take that message and proclaim it to a lost and dying world.

Rev. Robert S. Beckett

CHAPTER 1

From Smoldering Embers to Revival Fire

*"For the Lord your God is a consuming fire, a
jealous God..." (Deuteronomy 4:24).*

*"Therefore, since we are receiving a kingdom which cannot be shaken,
let us have grace, by which we may serve God acceptably with reverence
and godly fear. For our God is a consuming fire." (Hebrews 12:29).*

The fire had long died out in the church that I found myself called to. The minister leading the church was honoring the founding pastor who had died after 41 years of ministry. This interim pastor did nothing to rekindle that fire, he even admitted to me later, that he was "allowing them to mourn." Let me say this, there is a time for mourning, but no one can stay in that and remain healthy (Ecclesiastes 3:4). For three years the church was in this dark and sad state. In my spirit, as he was making that statement, I felt a checking of the Holy Spirit in me saying that things could not remain that way. To be fair to him the decline started long before he even came to fill in for the founding pastor that had been sick for at least 10 years off and on. With his 10-year illness, many things started to wane, attention that had been given before could not get the same amount of attention now. He was no longer a young man, full of energy and excitement. The mind and heart were willing, but the aging body was weak. Preparation of worship, messages, follow-up, and ministry in general suffered and in turn, the congregation suffered also. The heyday had long passed by a couple of decades, but the key members hung in there and remained.

As my wife and I walked into the building to interview, as a pastoral candidate, the feeling of the surroundings was dark and gloomy. I almost feel bad saying this, but the place looked and felt like a funeral home more than a place of worship. The lighting was low and dim, because many of the flickering florescent lights needed bulbs replaced. Maintenance had not been kept up with and most rooms in the building were used as storage because the children's Sunday School room had not been used in years. It was very easy to see that the fire had died many years before this moment had come. There were many other things about that day and the weeks to follow but we will be discussing those in chapters to come.

I think for me the most glaring and obvious sign that the embers were but a smolder in that little church, was the spirit of hopelessness of the leaders that had tirelessly struggled to hang on for so long. They were tired and at their wits end on what to do. I know that the word hopeless and despair should not ever be associated with a church, because Christ is the Head of the Church, but this is the case for many churches today and not just this church. People can be hung out like an old dishrag, and they feel as if they have nothing hardly left in the tank after so many weary years without seeing any measurable result at all.

Here is the most important part of the story of this church…they did not want to remain this way. They were not ready to give up and give in. This group of leaders wanted to do whatever they could to bring fire and life back to this small church that they loved so much. They did not know at the time what that would mean for them and what it would cost, but they were willing to go forward.

George Barna says that " a church cannot be turned around until a contingent (or remnant) of the people is so firmly committed to the ministry of the church that they will sacrifice almost anything for the good of the church, to the glory of God." It is no wonder that so many churches are struggling, the fire in the church has turned to smoldering ashes. Until the people of the church receive and recognize the vision and purpose that God has for that local congregation, nothing of any significance will happen. Bringing the church back to revitalization requires obedience to God's vision. Church leaders or committees can develop a multitude of programs and activities. They can invest all kinds of money to make these productions or projects attractive and appealing. But human effort equals human results which is inadequate compared to God's effort and God's intended results. There is the answer to the problem, God must provide the fire. We must turn to the Father for our every need. Things may seem difficult for your church, but they are not impossible because God is on your side. God will help you and your church if we allow Him to rule and reign.

I am reminded of Leviticus 6:13 which says, *"A fire shall always be burning on the altar; it shall never go out."* This is the root of the problem plaguing most churches facing a decline. They do not tend the fire. One definition of "tend" is to apply oneself to the care of or to have or take charge of as a caretaker or overseer. God is telling the church that we must take care of, and stoke the heavenly fire that the Holy Spirit provides and brings to us. But we can be neglectful, and distracted, taking our eyes off the vision that God provides for us. When this happens, we must seek to rekindle those fires in our church. Somewhere in the beginning history of your church, the church that you attend or lead, someone had a vision and fire that God placed in them to start that church, in that place, at that time. It is time to reestablish and rekindle that fire. At some point, God placed a vision, and a burning desire in someone to start the church that you are leading now, to do ministry right there, in that spot. Often over time, that fire may grow cold or completely die out. But as long as you are seeking His will and being obedient to His instruction then the fire can be rekindled there. It can start with you.

There are many factors that are involved in a church that has lost its fire. It doesn't happen overnight or by deliberate decisions of neglect or disobedience. It can happen from time, routine, distractions, satisfaction with status quo, people getting older, and simply being tired from many years of work. No one consciously chooses to grow cold; it moves in slowly and without much notice. John records in Revelation 3:1-3

"These things says He who has the seven Spirits of God and the seven stars: "I know your works, that you have a

name that you are alive, but you are dead. Be watchful, and strengthen the things which remain, that are ready to die, for I have not found your works perfect before God. Remember therefore how you have received and heard; hold fast and repent. Therefore, if you will not watch, I will come upon you as a thief, and you will not know what hour I will come upon you."

"Be watchful and strengthen the things that remain" is the key to the whole problem. Jesus says, *"I know your works."* They were still doing things, but not the things that deliver life to them because Jesus continues by saying, *"you have a reputation of being alive, but you are dead"* like a coal removed from the fire. (Emphasis added).

Starting and keeping a fire can be difficult work but the reward for such work can be unbelievable. There must be the right conditions and appropriate material for a fire to be strong and to burn hot. The wood must first be dry, not damp or wet for a fire to take off. Have you ever heard the phrase, "I don't want to pour water on his or her wood", meaning they don't want to be an obstacle or hindrance to the plans of someone else. Anyone building a fire knows that you must start with dry kindling that will take the flame easily.

The kindling must be in small pieces so that the flame catches quickly and easily. Starting with highly combustible material will give a good start and a higher success rate for a good fire. So, in church life, small steps and small wins help to fuel the flame in any church regardless of the size. Making yourself highly combustible for God is done through much prayer, reading the living word of God to know His heart, and being sensitive to the Holy Spirit moving and stirring your heart. These things will create a good fire starter in you for God to use. Examples of small church wins might be the congregation coming together to clean up the church property and fixing neglected repairs that needed to be done years ago. Fresh paint on tired walls, washing dirty windows, pulling the weeds around the church sign, and replacing those flickering fluorescent lights with LEDs can cause a spark of excitement to occur. What happens is the congregation can renew a fresh sense of honoring God with excellence in the church property. It all starts with small steps.

A small step might be starting with a neighborhood cookout. Most guys have a grill around the house. Put some hamburgers or hot dogs on the grill and invite anyone passing by to eat with you. Small things can lead to big results. Church yard sales are great ways to make connection points with the community and benefit the church at the same time. Don't just make it a revenue source but use it as a way to interact with others and even possibly create relationships with people that you didn't know before. It is a great way to open doors to conversations about who you are and what you are doing. It has never failed that each time we as a church has held a yard sale someone has always asked about the church, times of service and what we believe. Small things can start bigger things with the right fuel for the fire. You are the fuel that God wants to use.

Fire Starter Moments

Only God knows where we will make contacts that will make a difference for the Kingdom. One small example of how God can take a small thing and create something beautiful out of it was at a pig roast that the church held for the community. We roasted a whole pig on the traditional roasting rotisserie and invited the community to come and eat with us. Many people came, including the Fire Department, police, and anyone else that wanted to come enjoy.

One of those that came that day was Rosie. Rosie was a neighbor of the church that lived in the senior apartment complex directly behind the church. We had never met her before but because of the pig roast, in her own words, "Maybe I'll go check these people out," and that is just what she did.

That event was on a Saturday, and because of the people she talked to and the feeling of welcoming conversation, she started coming to the church that Sunday. Rosie became a faithful and devoted member of the church. Rosie loved our church and loved our people but loved God most of all. She passed away a couple of years ago, but she made an impression upon all of us because we still make mention of her often in conversations. You never know what God may use to make a connection for your church, it may even be a pig.

Building the Fire

So, the bigger the flame of any fire gets then the bigger the wood that goes on the fire. Small steps lead to bigger steps. Bigger steps could include VBS for children or intentional outreach opportunities like volunteering in community events that already exist. You could be part of the volunteer force in local parades, city, and county fairs, set up church booths at local events, and find ways to become part of the fabric of the community that the church is in.

There is a natural progression to building a fire. The more fuel that is added to the flame, the hotter it becomes. As you add wood and oxygen, the fire grows larger and blazes stronger. The same is true of the fire within the church congregation. The more obedience and faithfulness the congregation finds itself rediscovering and displays in following God's leading, the more rampant the flames spread throughout the church. The beautiful thing about this fire is that the more it burns in the church, the more that it is recognized by the community that is around it. When fires take off everyone takes notice. It can be like fire in a windstorm, spreading fast and wide. People take notice of the glow of great fires, and they take notice of the heat that is emitted from them. God's holy fire is no different. When the fire is hot and burning in the church then people take notice of what God is doing and cannot help but to be affected by its warming glow.

So how and why is the fire so important and essential for the life of a church? In Leviticus, it is mentioned several times that the fire in the altar was to burn continuously. God wanted a perpetual fire burning there, and He must have had a very good reason for it to remain.

1. **The Fire was the Very Representation of God Himself.** Before the law was ever given, God appeared to Moses *"And the Angel of the Lord appeared to him in a flame of fire from the midst of a bush.*

So, he looked, and behold, the bush was burning with fire, but the bush was not consumed." (Exodus 3:2). God chose the appearance of a continuous fire when calling Moses to lead the people out of Egypt to a new land. Later, when God was leading the Israelites out of Egypt, God appeared as a pillar of fire at night (Exodus 13:21–22). Then came the Law. Outside the tabernacle, the fire for the burnt offering was commanded to be kept burning; never was it to be extinguished. Leviticus 6:13 instructs, *"A fire shall always be burning on the altar; it shall never go out."* This is mentioned three times in this chapter (verses 9, 12, and 13). Churches today can try to create an atmosphere of emotional and spiritual awakening, but nothing will replace The Almighty Himself in your church through the Holy Spirit. When the fire of God is burning fast and hot in a church then God is the one recognized as the source. When the church is on fire for God, it will be a place where His presence is felt strongly. It will be a place of miracles, signs, and wonders. People will be transformed by the power of God and lives will be changed forever. This is the kind of church that Jesus is coming back for! Do you want your church to be on fire for God? Then let us pray that the Holy Spirit will fall fresh on your church and ignite a mighty revival!

2. **The Fire was the Demonstration of His Power.** Another reason the ongoing fire was so important is that it was started directly by God: *"and fire came out from before the Lord and consumed the burnt offering and the fat on the altar. When all the people saw it, they shouted and fell on their faces."* (Leviticus 9:24). So, for this reason, the fire on the altar served as a constant reminder of God's power. It was a manifestation from heaven. No other source of the fire was acceptable to God. The church can try to manufacture and duplicate but nothing other than the real fire that only can come from God will work for your church. The manifestation of the Holy Spirit in having free reign in the people and in the services will only do for God. Be like the 120 in the upper room and pray and wait for God to bring the fire. With sincere hearts and surrendered wills, God will show up and start a fire in you.

The fire was the demonstration of God's power. It was a sign that He was with the Israelites and would protect them from their enemies. The fire also showed His glory and majesty, and His love for His people.

3. **The Fire Also Represented God's Presence.** *"For the Lord your God is a consuming fire, a jealous God"* (Deuteronomy 4:24). The Shekinah glory was visible in the fire at the altar of burnt offering. Shekinah glory is a form of a Hebrew word that literally means "he caused to dwell," signifying that it was a divine visitation of the presence or dwelling of the Lord God on this earth in their place of standing. This ongoing presence of God reminded the Israelites that salvation is of the Lord. The atonement made at the burnt offering could only be made through Him. In our churches, we must allow and tend to the fire and presence of God in our church life throughout our services, our ministries, and our church fellowship. The fire must not go out for any reason or everything we do as a church will be hollow and shallow. The fire of the Holy Spirit was said to have descended on the day of Pentecost, and this event was considered to be the birth of the church. The fire also appeared at various other important moments in early Christian history, such as when Constantine had his vision of the cross.

    The fire represented God's presence in a very real way for early Christians. It was a tangible sign that God was with them, and that He was involved in their lives. The fire was a constant reminder of His presence and His power, and it served as a source of strength and comfort for believers.

4. **The Fire Represented the Purity of God.** In the New Testament, John the Baptist said that the Messiah would baptize with the Spirit and with fire (Matthew 3:11; Luke 3:16). Fire serves as a sign of judgment and refining, but it also reminds us of the Holy Spirit's coming at Pentecost in the form of *"tongues of fire"* (Acts 2:3). What our plateauing and declining churches need is a renewed and rekindled pure fire that only the Holy Spirit can bring. Churches are smoldering embers, shadows of past glory, dying out because of one reason, or for many. They have been

reduced to ashes. We need to expose ourselves to the consuming fire of God and allow Him to burn away anything that is not like Him in our churches. Like David, in Psalms 51:10 he asked God to create in him a new heart. Let the purifying fire of God help us to be found faultless before Him.

The continuously burning, divine fire at the altar of burnt offering helped remind the Israelites of the reality of God's presence and of their need for God. The sacred fire endured throughout the 40 years in the desert and likely beyond that, as tabernacle worship continued until the time of King Solomon and the building of the Jewish temple. When the temple was dedicated, God once again lit the fire on the altar (2 Chronicles 7:1).[1] Let us, let God, light the fire in and on us again. The same way that He did when your church first started. May the remnant of people in your church start praying and seeking the fire from heaven that only God can provide for you. May the fire get inside each and every person in such a way that they will be willing to do anything that God commands of them and they will do it without abandon. May it be a continually burning fire that is from God. May your church be the continual burning fire that cannot be put out, instead always tended to, and stoked. May the fire that comes to your church reflect His appearance, demonstrate His power, manifest His presence, and most of all cleanse and purify each and every one for the furtherance of His Glorious Kingdom.

The Holy Fire of God can burn away sin and rebellion, but it also brings the purity of new life. Of all God's many wonderful attributes, there is nothing that can compare to the splendor and beauty of His all-consuming holiness. That means holiness is chief among His attributes. This is the reason the angels, 24 elders, the 4 creatures, and the multitude all cried Holy, Holy, Holy throughout eternity. That means His character is perfect in every single way. He is the very definition of purity. God's supreme holiness infinitely sets Him apart from His creation. Therefore, having His Holy Fire in us and in our churches is the most extraordinary possession that we can have burning in our lives.

Telling Our Story

What is the story of your church? I can confidently guarantee that the beginning story of your church, regardless of the age, started with some people coming together with a fire in their belly that God had placed in them to plant that church right there, in that spot. It is most certainly a story of energy and excitement for the work that God wanted them to do. It is time to regain that energy and excitement now for what God has for your church now. There is not a church on the face of the earth that has not got a plan and a purpose for them to accomplish where they are at. What we must do is rekindle the fire back in and on our church to fulfill that plan and mission. We must be willing to allow God to place His Holy Fire upon the altar of our lives and of the church. Not allowing the fire to go out. Allowing God to burn in such a way that everyone to see.

These are some of the very reasons for this book. It is to let you and your church know that you are not alone, and you are not in this by yourself. Although the source is unknown, there is a little story that I think will help illustrate the principle behind the ember and the fire.

The Separated Coal

A member of a certain church, who previously had been attending services regularly, stopped going. After a few weeks, the pastor decided to pay the fellow a visit. It was a chilly evening in early winter. The pastor upon arriving, found the man at home alone, sitting before a blazing fire.

Guessing the reason for his pastor's visit, the man welcomed him in, led him to a big chair near the fireplace, and waited for the question that was sure to come, "why he had not been to services as of late?" The pastor made himself comfortable in the chair but said nothing. In the grave silence, he contemplated the play of the flames around the burning logs in the fireplace.

After some minutes, the pastor took the fire tongs and carefully picked up a brightly burning ember and placed it on one side of the hearth all alone. Then he sat back in his chair, still silent not saying a word. The fellow watched all this in quiet fascination. Watching rather intently, they both observed that the one lone ember's flame diminished, there was a momentary glow and then its fire was no more. Soon it was cold and "dead as a doornail."

Not a word had been spoken since the initial greeting. Just before the pastor was ready to leave, he picked up the cold, dead ember and placed it back in the middle of the fire. Immediately it began to glow once more with the light and warmth of the burning coals around it. As the pastor got out of the chair and reached for the door to leave, his host said, "Thank you so much for your visit and especially for the fiery sermon. I shall be back in church next Sunday."

Staying in the midst of the fire is vital for the well-being of the churchgoer but even more so for the church body. The Fire of God needs to be tended to and cared for in our presence and never allowed to go out or we will start to die and grow cold. The lack of fire in the church is a result of neglect and not keeping first things first.

You can do this. If there is a desire and longing for the fire of God in your life and church life, then there is hope. That hope is the God All-Mighty living in you and your church body. Start fanning those embers that remain and fanning them in such a way that the embers get hotter and hotter to the point of flame again. Start adding kindling as the flame grows. God wants your church to be everything that He has intended for you from the beginning.

Reflection Questions

1. How is the fire that is in your church? Is there a fire at all? Has your fire turned into smoldering ashes?
2. Has there been any major difficulties or challenges that has caused your fire to wane?
3. Have you become cold and complacent in your service to God?
4. What is it going to take for your church to regain the fire of God in your congregation?

Best Practices/Ideas

1. The absolute first place for revitalization is within us. Repenting and recognizing that the fire must start within our lives and devotion for the God-given fire. We are the carriers of the needed flame. The fire must be burning fully in us before it can burn anywhere else.

2. Recognizing the need for the flame of revitalization in your church. Corporately repenting and admitting there is a problem is part of the first step.

3. Take small steps of obedience to point you in the right direction. Doing the small things will help build confidence and boldness to take the bigger steps.

4. Look for opportunities to connect with your neighbors around you. Let the church be the best neighbor the community has.

5. Your church does not always have to start a new thing but to get involved in things already going on in your community. That can be your first small step.

6. Go and volunteer to help at feeding programs in the community. Even if it is at another church of another denomination.

7. Have a yard sale with the intention of making connections with the shoppers. Have printed material about your church and services to give to everyone that comes. Have people there with the sole purpose to mingle and starting conversations.

CHAPTER 2

Am I Really the One to Lead This Revitalization Effort?

"But he said, "O my Lord, please send by the hand of whomever else You may send."
(Exodus 4:13)

Also, I heard the voice of the Lord, saying: "Whom shall I send, and who will go for Us?" Then I said, "Here am I! Send me."
(Isaiah 6:8)

When I came to pastor this little church, I did not know everything that I was walking into, but I knew this, if something did not happen soon the church was going to close. In many ways, I was like Moses, thinking I was not prepared for the task at hand, but God showed me something very early in the ministry here. I did not need to know every turn and decision that was going to have to be made to lead this church in the right direction, I did need to be obedient in what step He has called me to take. I did not need to know the destination He was leading, but to hear Him and take that one step right then. The beautiful thing I finally realized after trusting and stepping for some time, was that I will end up in the right place every time because I let Him lead and not me.

I am not sure but maybe the good thing about a church that is at the end of the rope is we must trust God and quit coming up with excuses as to why we cannot do things that He has called us into. I believe the biggest excuse that we still must fight, is the excuse that we are too old, or we are too small. There is a tremendous temptation to fall back on that excuse because it seems easy and logical…just look at us. But that is not what God sees. God wants to see a people that are obedient in all things and through that obedience, He will bless and part waters before us.

I remember very clearly the first board meeting I had as the pastor of this church. The six of us sat around a fold-up table in the sanctuary because the office of the founding pastor was locked and never used. In the 3 years since his passing it was full of clutter, cobwebs, and dead crickets all over the floor. In the meeting, I expressed to them the thanks I had for the opportunity to lead and pastor this church and the hopes and prayers that I had for us all. Since it was our first meeting, it did not take long for us to get into the meat of the meeting…what was the state of the finances of the church? To be frank, there was not much to talk about. The church was flat busted broke. The general fund was so low they had to take out of the building fund to pay the liability insurance for the property. After that we had just enough left to pay maybe one more quarter and that was it. They were literally down to the last nickels to rub together before they ran out of money. The church operated a daycare that paid the church utilities and phone bills to keep it afloat. Fortunately, the church had a property that was purchased many years before by the late pastor. We were able to sell the property to an interested member, which gave some income to the church to help sustain it for some time till we could get things back on track.

In that board meeting, looking at the financial report, I saw that certain obligations had not been made to the denomination or the district for some time. The response was that they decided not to pay for those things because they did not have enough money to do so. It is so easy to get caught up in the excuses that we don't have enough of this or that, but we are to be faithful people in all things and not just a few or selected things. With understanding and consideration in my heart for their concern, I let them know that from that point on we would fulfill our obligations and that we would always work toward that goal.

We could have had many good excuses not to do certain things in and around the church but letting our obedience dominate and override our excuses will push us toward our mission and commission by God.

I imagine this question has run across the mind and lips of just about every pastor and leader that has ever found themselves in a place of revitalization at one time or another. "Am I really the one to lead this revitalization effort?" Or better yet, "Lord, I don't know that I can do this." The answer to those questions and more is "No, you are not the one," but our Lord and Savior Jesus Christ is. But you are the one He wants to use in this revitalization.

The Holy Spirit provides the fire needed to ignite us, but we do have a part to play. As pastors and leaders, we are to tend the fire, stoking and fanning the flame in the church. We are to bring kindling to add to it. In scripture, we get this idea that we are to contribute to the fire that God brings to the church. After the shipwreck on the Island of Malta, Paul and his companions were welcomed by the local Maltese people (who are still very well known for their hospitality). They lit a bonfire to warm up the shipwrecked travelers. Paul, caring less for his own comfort than the comfort of his companions, decided not to sit by the fire but rather he wanted to serve by collecting kindling for the fire with the locals. The only way any church can sustain the fire that God lights in their church is for everyone to bring fuel for the fire. Everyone must do their part to contribute and serve. Many churches that are plateauing and declining bring excuses rather than fuel for the fire, trying to excuse themselves from not doing the work of the church body. Pastor and leaders, do not just sit there, do something to contribute to the work of God. We are called, as people and leaders, to add to the fire that God is building in your church. As a called leader of a church, God wants you to lead well by example.

Too many churches are sitting on the edge of a great move of God yet are hindered by their "buts." Here are the Ten Most Used Excuses to not contribute:

1. I forgot.
2. No one told me to go ahead.
3. I didn't think it was that important.
4. Wait until the boss comes back and ask him.

5. I didn't know you were in a hurry for it.
6. That's the way we've always done it.
7. That's not my department.
8. How was I to know this was different?
9. I'm waiting for an O.K.
10. That's his job—not mine.

When God appeared to Moses at the burning bush...He called him to the task of leading the children of Israel out of Egyptian bondage. In response, Moses gave his reasons why he did not think he was the man for the job. The "buts" of Moses, and God's response to them, will serve as the basis for our thoughts today...

For in a similar way, as God's people today, we have received a special calling. Not to go out to a country to deliver those in physical bondage but rather the world, to deliver those in the bondage of sin (Mk 16:15;1Pe 2:9-10). Too often, though, we behave just like Moses, making the very same excuses! Let us consider the first of five "buts" given by Moses...

I. **"WHO AM I?" (Exodus 3:11).** Though Moses was once a member of the ruling house of Egypt, he was now but a lowly shepherd. It had been forty years since he had been in Egypt. He was now an 80-year-old man, already past the average lifespan of his generation. This prompted Moses to wonder whether he was the right man for the job. But God's response was quick and should have been adequate..."I will certainly be with you..." (Exodus 3:12). God promised to be with Moses, and this alone should have been sufficient. As Paul later wrote, "If God is for us, who can be against us?" (Romans 8:31).

    For churches today, many times we live shallow, puny lives because we do not or will not recognize that we are called by God Almighty, Creator of the Universe, to step out, not on our own, but with Him and for Him. What God has asked us to do He will equip us to do. God has your back. You can step out in courage because with His help we can accomplish what He has set before us. You are not alone in this revitalization effort. You are the instrument and vessel that God wants to use for His glory. Within ourselves, we can do nothing but with God all things are possible.

II. **"WHAT SHALL I SAY?" (Exodus 3:13).** Moses knew that when he went to the children of Israel, there were bound to be questions. Such as, "Who is this God who sent you to us?" And perhaps, "Why are we to leave this country we have come to consider our home for over 400 years?" Moses expresses inadequacy in knowing what to say but again, God's response was quick..."Thus you shall say..." – (Exodus 3:14). God tells Moses what he needs to say in response to their questions.

We try to excuse ourselves by saying that our knowledge is inadequate, but God has told us what to say...It is really quite simple. How simple? (1Corinthians 15:3-4) *"For I delivered to you first of all that which I also received: that Christ died for our sins according to the Scriptures, and that He was buried, and that He rose again the third day according to the Scriptures."* Paul also said, *"For I determined not to know anything among you except Jesus Christ and Him crucified."* We do not need to add anything of our own words to the Gospel of Jesus Christ. The Scripture tells us everything that we need to say. That Jesus came, lived, died, and rose again for our deliverance from sin. There is nothing more to add.

And so, as with Moses, we have no reason for saying "what shall I say?" God will give the thing to say at the right time with the right words that are needed for that moment. As we return to Moses, we see that despite God instructing him what to say, he soon raises the third objection.

III. **"SUPPOSE THEY WILL NOT BELIEVE ME?" (Exodus 4:1).** Now that he knows what to say, he balks at the idea that the people may not listen. Is he afraid of failing? Has he already forgotten that God will be with him? God responds by equipping him with several convincing proofs...The rod, which turns into a serpent (Exodus 4:2-5), His own hand, which turns into leprosy (Exodus 4:6-8), The water, which will turn to blood when dropped on the dry ground (Exodus 4:9).

What will it take to convince you that God means business? What does He have to do to you or for you to know that what He has asked you to do is real? Are you afraid of rejection and looking foolish to others? Jesus told us that if and when we are rejected that it is actually Him that they are turning their backs on. They are rejecting the message.

IV. **"I AM SLOW OF SPEECH AND SLOW OF TONGUE" (Exodus 4:10).** Moses claims that he is not an eloquent speaker, but God is not disturbed by this objection...He already knows the inability of those He calls (Exodus 4:11). God is able to make up for anyone's shortcomings. Again, promising to be with Moses (Exodus 4:12), He had even arranged for Aaron to be Moses' mouthpiece.

Some try to use these "buts" today, but God uses those like Uncle Bud Robinson (1890-1930), who stuttered, was uneducated, and suffered epileptic seizures. Yet he was a powerhouse for evangelism and preached at least 500 times a year. God wants to use you where He has placed and called you to.

We have considered four "buts" that Moses gave; but as mentioned earlier, they were really smokescreens. The true reason for all these "buts" is revealed in Exodus 4:13...

V. **"PLEASE SEND...WHOMEVER ELSE YOU MAY SEND" MOSES SIMPLY DID NOT WANT TO GO!** The previous "buts" were simply a smokescreen attempt to hide this fact! Now that the smokescreen is removed, God's impatience with Moses becomes evident. His anger was kindled against Moses (Exodus 4:14a). Read verses 15-17 with an emphasis on the word "shall" to appreciate the anger of the Lord.[1]

THE SAME IS TRUE WITH US TODAY! Any and every excuse we could offer is only a smokescreen. We really want God to use someone else! We really don't want to do what God has called us to do! But my friends, the anger of the Lord is kindled against those who do not live up to their calling!

If we have been making excuses, we need to repent! Let me encourage you today, God is prepared for any obstacle that you may feel lays ahead, God has made provision for you and is ready to equip you for the task.

It is no surprise that God uses reluctant and common people to accomplish some of the greatest displays of His awesomeness and wonder. I believe it is a fair question to ask God why you, why now, and why in this place? Let's face it, I don't care how equipped you may feel, or how fluent you may be in the latest revitalization books. You can sit in seminar after seminar. We are human and have human inadequacies. We must rely on God to supply everything we need. Like Moses, we must be secure in knowing the fact that God said, "I will be with you..." the minister's response to a call to ministry and especially a call to revitalization, is a response to God's call. Ministry is a response to an invitation outside of ourselves. We must realize God qualifies the called! We are here, the leadership of God's people, because we have responded to a summons because we were sought, called, sent, commissioned by one greater than ourselves, that our lives might be expended on work more significant than ourselves." [1]

It is this calling from God that provides us with the direction and strength to continue in the work even when we feel inadequate and spent to our wit's end. God is the one that directs our paths in every endeavor, but I believe especially in revitalization. It has made me realize that I must rely and depend upon the Holy Spirit to direct my every step in all aspects of my ministry and life in general.

Fire Starter Moments

When I became a pastor in the Kentucky district, I started pastoring the Nazarene church in a small town just south of Louisville. I became a pastor at a very late stage in life at the age of 51, Unlike many my age, I didn't have the knowledge or experience under my belt. Instead, I pray every day that God would direct my steps one at a time. I only asked for the step in front of me because that was the most important one at that moment. I didn't worry about 3, 7, or 10 steps ahead because I couldn't get there until I took one in front of me. I live all aspects of my life and ministry this way. I often confess to people that I have no idea how I'm supposed to be a pastor except for God showing me one step at a time. Here is the sweet blessing of living and ministering in this way, if I take each step He shows me, one at a time, then I will end up where He wants me and the congregation every single time because I wait on Him. We must have complete reliance upon Him and not on our own understanding. John Wesley said regarding accepting the call of God is that we are, "ready to do anything, to lose anything, to suffer anything." God has placed us where we are for a purpose and reason.

Dr. David F. Nixon wrote about the subject of leadership, which not only applies to pastors in general but to revitalization pastors particularly. He wrote "Ten Affirmations of the Called,"[2]

1. I will be attentive to God in prayer, Scripture reading, and in spiritual direction.
2. I will be faithful to my calling when I see no visible results of my efforts, and when I have no sense that people are getting better because of my work. I will seek God's help to be faithful to God's calling.
3. I will keep my soul on fire, and will not base my work on feelings, but on God's faithfulness.
4. I will recall the joy of being grasped by something greater than myself, namely, my vocation.
5. To those who count me a fool to pursue the heavenly vision, I respond with Nehemiah, "I am engaged in a great work and refuse to stop" (Nehemiah 6:3).
6. I have been called by the Spirit of God working in me, to a representative ministry within the people of God.
7. I am to lead God's people in worship and prayer and to nurture, teach and encourage Your people from the riches of God's grace.
8. I will exemplify Christ's servanthood; I will build up the people of God in their obedience to Christ's mission in the world; I will seek justice, peace, and salvation for all people.
9. It is my job to proclaim by word and deed the gospel of Jesus Christ, to lead persons to faith in Jesus Christ, and to conform their lives in accordance with the gospel.

10. I am called to serve rather than to be served, to proclaim the faith of the Church and no other, to look after the concerns of Christ above all.

Recognizing and acknowledging that God is the one in control of all things, especially the work of revitalization, will help us keep perspective. Knowing that God is on the Throne and is in total control, relieves us of the responsibility of the work before us and places the responsibility in the correct place, which is with God. The Father already knows what He wants of you, the pastor and leader, and what He wants for your congregation and community. Trusting and resting on that promise will free us to receive direction and guidance from the Holy Spirit to do the work that is laid before us. There can be freedom knowing that the work before us is God's.

Telling Our Story

I knew very early that something needed to happen that would encourage and lift the spirit of defeatism in the church. We needed to do something, regardless of how small, to help give some life to this beaten-down congregation. The church leadership decided to do a movie night/block party for the community to let them know that we are still here and that we are still alive. We contacted a company for bounce houses, a fire department for fire trucks, and police department to mingle and provide security. We reached out to the local pharmacy, children's dental office, and the local children's hospital. They all came and set up booths and gave away prizes to the children. We then showed one of the recently released kid's movies and showed it free of charge to everyone!

Here we are a church that only a few months earlier was near shutting down and now we are doing a completely free community event. It was amazing the response and interaction we had during that event. At best count we had 450 people come through our event.

I thought that it might spark community interest in our church and in attendance, but what happened was the church was sparked by the community and it helped start a fire in them. They could now see that there was hope and a future for this congregation if we would only be obedient and not let our excuses get in the way. We must be very careful not to let the failure of nerves or the failure of the heart take us over.

God has a call for every individual and for every church. As He did for Moses, God will help and provide for you that He has called you into. God will not leave you in the lurch. Trust that God will do what He says He will do without all the excuses of Moses. God equips the one that He calls. You can do this because God called you there. Let go and let God.

I think Dr. Nixon said well, as a pastor or leader, that we need to continue in the work that God called us into, regardless of the lack of evidence of results or that the people were not getting it. That we must remain faithful to this call because God is always faithful to us. Pastor, keep plugging along faithful and true to the vision that God placed in you. The results are for Him and not for us.

Reflection Questions

1. What is it that God has called you into and you have come up with every reason you can think of not to do it?
2. Can you find the courage to step out and say here I am? If not, why?
3. Can you take that first step of obedience and then the next?

Best Practices/Ideas

1. Go to prayer today and ask God for the strength and courage to step out. He wants to do that for you, and He is waiting for you to make that first move.
2. Examine and see where you have been making excuses and determine to exchange those excuses for obedience.
3. Write on paper the areas you know God wants to move in your life and ministry so you can look at them and pray about them.
4. I highly recommend that you find someone that you can talk to and get yourself a spiritual tune-up. Someone that is distant

enough away from where you are ministering but close enough
that they can relate and encourage with "been there, done that"
experience.

5. Keep in the front of your mind that this is the work of God and
not yours. You are the instrument, and He holds the responsibility
of the plan. You hold the responsibility of serving and not to be
served.

CHAPTER 3

Your Perception of The Church Must Change

*And the man said to me, "Son of man, look with your eyes and hear
with your ears, and fix your mind on everything I show you; for
you were brought here so that I might show them to you. Declare
to the house of Israel everything you see."" (Ezekiel 40:4)*

*"Then He put His hands on his eyes again and made him look up.
And he was restored and saw everyone clearly." (Mark 8:25)*

It is sad that some would choose to walk the familiar path rather than
the "old path" that God established for us. In our church, like many
others, some preferred the path of comfort and tradition wanting to come
"do" church like they had become accustomed to for so many years before.
They are trapped in nostalgia and reminiscing their lives away. Nostalgia
is a silo that will lock you into the same old thing because we have always
done this same old thing for so many years. A silo of going in circles but
making no forward progress.

Breaking that circling path to nowhere must start somewhere. That
somewhere and sometime is now. There will always be some that will
refuse to leave their silos. We can try to show them and convince them
that it is healthier for the whole church if they get out of the trap, but the
choice is ultimately theirs to make. In our church, this moving forward
was a must. The church was dying at a rate that was unsustainable. Not all
at once, but some left because it was more than they could take. They did

not storm out in a rage, but eased out, becoming less involved, attendance became erratic, and finally reached the point of not coming back.

Any loss is hard and unwanted. When a church breaks out of the silo there will be some that leave the church. You try to encourage them, hoping that they see what God is doing with the church and decide to come along for the journey, but some will not. Regardless, we must move forward for the Kingdom work that is before us. Pastors and leaders, once you have the church moving forward you cannot allow anyone to keep you from continuing onward. Loss is the greatest struggle for anyone to deal with, but I guarantee there will be loss along the way. You must push through those times with even more determination and resolve.

What is Reality?

Everyone has his or her own perception of reality. The implication is that because each of us perceives the world through our own eyes, reality itself changes from person to person. While it's true that everyone perceives reality differently, the reality could care less about our perceptions. Your perception does not determine reality. Reality does not change to adapt to our viewpoints; reality is what it is: Reality is fact. Reality is truth. Reality, however, is not always tangible, which is where the perception of reality comes in. While reality is a fixed factor in the equation of life, perception of reality is a variable.[1]

Word association exercises are often good indicators of the mindset and worldview of the participants involved. Sociologists often uses this method to determine the thought process of their subjects. If you ask a group of people to express words that they would associate with small, you will get a wide range of responses. With most, if not all, the responses are negatively charged in the application. This should be of no surprise, for if someone would look up the word small in the dictionary, it has been portrayed negatively in each of the definitions. Definitions such as having a comparatively little size or slight dimensions; minor in influence, diminished power, or rank; little or close to zero in an objectively measurable aspect.

Business leaders know that the perception or reputation of their company has a lot to do with how they do business and impacts their bottom lines tremendously. Customers that have a particular perception of a company or product will many times determine if they will buy or choose to work with that company based on that perception. They will not investigate beyond their perception. Many times, people look at the church the same way. Because of past instances that have happened at the church regardless of the length of time that it has been, the reputation or perception of that church can be tarnished. Perhaps decades ago, the church had a split due to family feuds within the church. Maybe a pastor or one of the leaders of the church caused problems that became noticed by the community. There are churches that are known and perceived by the community, and even within the church community, as troubled churches that can't seem to keep pastors. It also becomes a real problem when the church and the leadership have skewed and diminished views of themselves. This just makes the problem even bigger. A wrong view of your church will distort and twist the perception that it has of its effectiveness and purpose. All these and more are contributing factors to the incorrect perception of the church.

It is no wonder that the small church struggles with the loss of identity and loss of purpose for themselves. If you would do the same word association exercise with "small church" you would get many of the same negative results: insignificant numbers, lack of money, handful of resources, inexperienced and entry-level pastors. Often people inside and outside the church define small churches by the numbers they have in attendance and in finances or even the lack of such resources. Numbers are most often used when judging the small church, pointing out its inadequacies or devaluing its effectiveness. This is a lie from the enemy. There is no church that is insignificant or worthless. The church's worthiness is not measured by our status or statistics, but worthiness comes from the cornerstone of our foundation which is Jesus Christ.

Small and rural churches are the backbone of the Church worldwide. Eight out of ten churches in the North American region are 100 or less in attendance. In the denomination in which I serve, in USA/Canada, there are just over 5000 churches; out of that 3800 are 100 or less (76%).

Thirty-three percent of the total giving was given by churches of 100 or less. These numbers go across the board regardless of the denomination that you belong to. Small and rural churches are vital for the furtherance of the Kingdom of God.

So why is it I feel insecure every time someone asks me how many people attend our church? Why do I think the success of my church is going to be judged by the number of people that attend? And why do I feel the urge to report higher numbers than I should? If you pastor a small church, be honest. You struggle with the same thoughts and questions. I believe it has to do with an identity crisis within ourselves and ultimately within our churches. The crisis is not that we don't know who we are, but that we forget Whose we are. We get so wrapped up in life and other distractions, that it causes us to forget that we belong to the Master of the universe. This plague of forgetting causes us to have the wrong perception of who we are. Turning our eyes upon Jesus and staying focused on Him is the only view that we should have, and the only one that will cure this ill.

What is your perception of your church? Perception, by definition, is a way of regarding, understanding or interpreting something, a mental impression. Perception is not necessarily reality. Perception acts as a lens through which we view reality. Our perceptions influence what we focus on, process, remember, interpret, understand, decide, and act on in our perceived reality. In doing so, our tendency is to assume that how we perceive reality is an accurate representation of what reality truly is.

Suppose two men are standing facing each other. They both are looking at the same thing written on the ground. One sees what looks to be a figure of a 6, but the other looks and sees a figure of a 9. Both are looking at the same thing but the perception of what they see is different for each of them. The same can go for your church. Some in your church can see one way but others can see another. If you would ask people "where do you go to church? Most of them that go to small rural communities would start off by saying, "We go to a small little church in so and so place with mostly an older congregation." The thing is, you did not ask them the size or the age of the congregation, but that is the information that they give you anyway. It is because they are subconsciously uncomfortable about who they are. Their perception is skewed. There is a feeling some think they must quantify their church's small status. Then usually they will go into the number of people that attend as if that was the question. I have been guilty of replying "I go to a little church of about 25 at so and so place" when asked where I attend church. They never asked that, but I felt I had to qualify my answer. Hey, may I remind you, it is God's church, and because of that, size does not matter…it does not make it insignificant. Every church everywhere has a purpose and mission to fulfill in its context. Your church is unique in its place. There is not another just like it. God prompted someone at some time to plant that church right there for a reason. Chances are that the need for starting that church in that place has not changed for the community, the church changed.

Another way we minimize our impact is by getting caught up in giving the membership number of the church when we are asked how many attend weekly, the reality is, that only a fraction show up on any given Sunday service. Somehow, by giving the larger membership number we are less ashamed of the real count. Our perception and thinking must change. Small is not a problem. What if our size is not the problem? What if when Jesus said "I will build my church" he had small rural churches in mind? What if Jesus' idea was for churches of all sizes to work together, big, small, and house churches each contributing something special to the whole church? What if by trying to fix a problem that isn't a problem, we are actually working against the strategy that God wants us to enact and fulfill? Have a strategy that sees our small churches as a vital tool to be used, and not a problem to be fixed or solved? What if God wants our church to be great instead of big?

Change from thinking of lack to thinking of supply

Great churches don't just happen by mistake. No matter what size they are. They take much prayer, planning, hard work, cooperation, and the calling of God. But no church can be a great church if they don't know they can be great in the first place. Small churches and their pastors are laboring under false pretenses, lies, and a foolish idea that their church can't be great until it becomes bigger. We need to put that lie of the enemy to rest, starting at the heart and ministry of every pastor of every small and rural church. So what, if there are lots of small country churches. So what, if our church is small? So what, if we are one of the denominations eighty percent? So what, if half of the people that go to church in our denomination go to small congregations instead of big ones? If they are faithful, reaching out to the lost, Jesus is being glorified, and we are doing Kingdom work, the size of the church should not matter?

We need new ways to look at church health and growth that go beyond numbers and counting people in the pews. The matrix of church health and growth needs to change and evolve to the environment that we now live in. We must be looking at measurements of health, vitality, outreach, and creating touchpoints.

Instead of saying our church is small, so what? We need to say our church is small, now what? What can we do with the resources we have now? There is a lot of ministries that can be done by churches while they are still small. Including things that can be done better because they are small. There are many reasons why a church may stay small but there is no reason a church should not be healthy. A healthy church seeks to increase its sending capacity rather than just its seating capacity. There are numerous churches that stay small but are setting a healthy example.

Planting churches. These churches set examples of sending and planting churches all around them. They are always looking for opportunities to plant in a new area.

Training churches. Small churches that are well suited to train and develop pastors during school years or an early ministry and offer internships during college. They are open to the idea of giving young and training ministers a chance to get experience in their church.

House churches. These are biblical examples of organic church plants. Meeting in each other's homes in a relaxed and intimate atmosphere.

Micro churches or PAC's. These are congregations that are sponsored by a parent congregation in places such as nursing homes, apartment complexes, coffee shops, etc.

There are plenty of reasons why churches may be small, but they can still be healthy churches, contributing to the Kingdom of God. We live in a culture that is so obsessed with a bigger is better mindset that we've allowed it to creep into the body of Christ. If many of the churches in the world are small, maybe we don't have a size problem as much as we have a health problem. Just imagine if every small church became healthy, strong, and vibrant. How would being small matter anymore? Changing our view to a healthy perception of ourselves would be a great place to start.

Recognizing our Identity and Purpose

Esteem has to do with identity and well-being; it is connected to the discovery or recovery of one's God-given individuality. If we do not understand who we are then we will not know what we are doing. This is the struggle for churches with such dynamics within its body. They see themselves as insignificant and many times impotent. Their self-esteem is negative and self-defeating. Psychologist Marsha Sinetar has this to say about the subject: "Self-esteem is just an idea we have about ourselves... about our competence, our worth, and our power...a picture we have in our minds about ourselves." She further suggests that "we often lose sight of our identity and self-esteem, or find it distorted, damaged, or hidden."

Often small churches, just like individuals, lose the image of themselves that God intended for them. They are swayed by the image dictated by peers, society as a whole and a culture that is dominating, an image backed by past failure and depression. The work before a church with this problem is to rediscover and capture that healthy God-given image that He intended and recover the small church's self-esteem and be transformed in it. Sinetar concludes: "[self-esteem is feelings] and self-pictures that we ourselves make real, and only we can change it for the better, for our own good, forever."

When identity is lost or distorted then the purpose is lost or distorted as well. The uncertainty of self can cause our purpose to drift from center, and left unchecked will lead to areas never intended to be dwelled in. No church happens accidentally. There is intention and purpose driving the new congregation of believers. But time seems to cause drift and slackness. We can become complacent in our worship, satisfied with tradition and the status quo. The fire in the belly grows cold without the coals being stoked like a blacksmith's furnace. The church finds itself saying, "we had no idea where we were going or what we were doing."

Who, Why, and How?

To truly understand their identity and purpose the church must discover the Who, Why, and How all over again. Paul tells us, *"Examine yourselves as to whether you are in the faith. Test yourselves. Do you not know yourselves, that Jesus Christ is in you?—unless indeed you are disqualified."* (2 Corinthians 13:5). We must take an honest look at ourselves to see if the fire that once burned within us has not dwindled down to a smoldering ember of what we once were.

Looking back to my childhood, one of the things I remember the most about the homeplace that I was raised in there was a cow pasture that ran with our property. I remember things like climbing the locust post fences, rolling rocks down the hill, and catching and playing with frogs in the natural spring that gave drink to the cattle. But probably the most memorable was walking and riding the cow paths along the hillside. There were many paths in that pasture, going in every direction. They all lead somewhere particular. They were going to the open fields full of green grass, or to the barn for shelter, or to the water source which was beside our house. Every path led to something good for them.

Allen Carr outlined in a sermon that God's people had badly missed the mark. He explained that in the days of Jeremiah's ministry to the people of Israel were days of deep spiritual wickedness. The people had sinned against God to the point where He was ready to give them up in captivity. And, in fact, they did go into captivity in just a few short years. Yet, even while they perched on the edge of judgment, the Lord desires to see them turn back to Him. In any church that is going through the process of the revitalization effort, churches are choosing to return to the old paths, established paths, which the Lord has laid out for them to walk.

"Thus says the Lord: "Stand in the ways and see, And ask for the old paths, where the good way is, And walk in it; Then you will find rest for your souls. But they said, 'We will not walk in it.'" (Jeremiah 6:16).

In this verse, we are given the image of a traveler who comes to a fork in the road. He has the opportunity to go any way he desires, but God tells him to ask for the "old paths, where is the good way". Instead of just traveling blindly on, this traveler is to stop and ask for directions. Many are too filled with pride to stop and ask, and as a result, they waste much valuable time seeking their own way. Any church that needs revitalization must ask for help. There is no shame in asking for help to turn your church around. God is a God of restoration, and He wants nothing more than to see your congregation healthy and happy serving the Lord to it's potential and ability. Of course, this is all in a religious context. The Lord wants His people to travel the right path. He wants them on a path that will lead them in His direction. While this word of correction was spoken to the Jews many years ago, there is a lesson in this verse for the modern revitalizing church today.

The Lord would still have His people ask for the old paths. Take a moment to consider the requirement, the reward, and the refusal as you "Ask for The Old Paths." There is a right path and there is a wrong path. We must be sure we are walking the one which God has ordained, the one that He can bless, the one that honors Him.

A Requirement

The command that God is issuing to His people is for them not to allow themselves to be led astray by the false prophets and leaders of their day. They are to look back to men like Abraham, Isaac, Jacob, Moses, and others who walked the path of obedience and holiness before the Lord, and they are to seek that path for themselves. God is wanting them to remember the fire that the church once had and the foundational things that their fathers did to have that zeal in their church. The foundations of the old established paths.

God's command is that they do not just go anywhere, but that they take the time to find the right path, that old, well-worn path that represents the best way. The problem Israel faced is a problem people have faced down through the ages. During World War II, during the Battle of the Bulge, there was a group of German soldiers who dressed in the uniforms of the Allies. These German soldiers used American military vehicles and went through the German countryside changing the road signs. When the American troops came to the various crossroads, they were often fooled and led off in the wrong direction. This deception by the Germans almost gave them the victory in this very decisive battle of the second world war.

Just like those German soldiers caused confusion and death by changing a few signs, so many in our day are leading churches into lives of cold embers with no heat of the fire, because they are changing some of the road signs of the faith. A few of the road signs are being changed in our day.[3]

1. **Salvation Through the Blood.** If a church uses worship songs that leave the blood out, then they are only singing part of the message. Good Friday they're probably singing plenty about the Cross, the death of Christ, salvation, grace, and related topics. But you're unlikely to sing about the blood of Christ. That's too bad, because as the old hymn goes, there is power in the blood. Read Hebrews 9:22 and it will plainly tell you, *"And according to the law almost all things are purified with blood, and without shedding of blood there is no remission."*

2. **Belief In the Scriptures.** People so water down and dissect the scriptures to suit their life that it does not have the authority and purifying fire that God intends. – *2 Tim. 3:16 "All Scripture is given by inspiration of God, and is profitable for doctrine, for reproof, for correction, for instruction in righteousness."*

3. **Love For the Church.** Churches are discontinuing Wednesday night prayer meetings, not doing any Sunday night services, no Sunday school, and only meeting for an hour on Sunday morning – one hour a week total. Scripture clearly tells us in *Hebrews 10:25 "not forsaking the assembling of ourselves together, as is the manner of some, but exhorting one another, and so much the more as you see the Day approaching."*

4. **The Reality of Heaven and Hell.** In *John 14:1-3 "Let not your heart be troubled; you believe in God, believe also in Me. In My Father's*

house are many mansions; if it were not so, I would have told you. I go to prepare a place for you. And if I go and prepare a place for you, I will come again and receive you to Myself; that where I am, there you may be also."

5. **The Value of The Human Soul.** *Mark 8:36-37 says, "For what will it profit a man if he gains the whole world, and loses his own soul? Or what will a man give in exchange for his soul?"*

6. **The Holiness of God.** We try to bring God down to man's level. He is holy. 1 Pet. 1:16 because it is written, *"Be holy, for I am holy."* The only way to bring back the consuming fire of God is to return to the old paths that God established long ago.

Regardless of which signs the world changes, it does not change the road! The Word of God is still settled in Heaven. We still know the "old paths". There is no question about which way is the right way. And God's requirement has not changed: ask for the old and walk therein!

A Reward

God's promise to those who walk in His paths is that they will find rest for our souls. That is, in His paths, we can be assured of three great truths. One truth that can be found in a cow's path is that it will find the route with the least resistance to travel. It will not go straight up the hill; it will be gradual and steady upward. We can be sure that we will arrive at the proper destination! When we take the Lord's highway, we can be sure that it will end in His presence! We can travel in safety knowing that the Lord is guarding our way. Not only will we end up where we want to be, but we will get there in the safest, most peaceful manner possible. We can know that while we are on the Lord's path, the deepest needs of our souls will be met! There will be fellowship with Him and joy in His presence at the end of the way! A truth that I learned in my childhood was that the cow's path will lead you to what you need. It will not lead to nowhere, it will lead to pasture fields, water troughs, or barns for shelter. Those who fail to ask for the old paths will find themselves walking in the ways of destruction and misery. When we turn our backs on the way God has chosen as the right way, we will find that the way is difficult, there is no peace or safety, and the destination is ever in question. There is a reward for those who will walk in the Lord's pathway! When we see ourselves as God intended for us to be then our twisted and distorted view of ourselves straightens and falls in line with how God sees us.

A Refusal

Jerimiah tells us that some decided that they would not walk in the Lord's will and in the Lord's path. The results of their choice are chastisement and destruction (Jerimiah 6:17-30). There is a high price to pay for refusing to walk in the Lord's will! We are living in a day when many are refusing to walk in the old paths. Either the old way is too narrow, or they feel that God just doesn't know what He is talking about. Yet, no matter what the world does, let us, the people of the Lord, stand tall in the old way. Let us be unashamed of who we are. Let us hold our heads high and walk in the way God has ordained without apology and without backing down. Let us be everything the Lord commanded us to be in His Word, *1 Cor. 15:58 "Therefore, my beloved brethren, be steadfast, immovable, always abounding in the work of the Lord, knowing that your labor is not in vain in the Lord."*[2]

For far too long the small church has bought a bill of goods that does not need to be true. They have bought into the assumption that since they are small then they must be insignificant. Small does not have to mean it is negative but that in fact, it is positive. The words that can accentuate the positive can be close, community, family, intimacy, and trusting are some of the things that can be said, but the potential is another. If you take a moment and think about the size of the church, then you can see that the small church has tremendous potential to do mighty things for God. The smallest obedient deed can be magnified because no one expects much from them. God receives multiplied glory in the midst of His small body of believers. The light is the brightest in the deepest darkness, even so, is God in the midst of His chosen few.

Telling Our Story

The story of our church is no longer a story of despair and hopelessness. God has shown up and demonstrated His wonderful acts of blessing upon us repeatedly. The members of the church and the people of the community see us as a place of hope and a place in which God dwells and works.

This is the story of how God has transformed our church. It is a story of hope and blessings. A story that demonstrates how, no matter what situation we find ourselves in, God can bring us through it if we trust and obey Him. Our church has been through some tough times recently. We have faced financial difficulties, been through some difficult transitions, and dealt with some serious challenges. But through it all, God has been faithful to us. He has provided for us, comforted us, and given us hope.

Now, we are a thriving community of faith. We are seeing new people joining our church all the time, and our congregation is growing. We are making a difference in our community, and we are seeing God work in powerful ways. This is the story of how God has transformed our church. It is a story of hope and blessings. A story that demonstrates how, no matter what situation we find ourselves in, God can bring us through it if we trust and obey Him.

Changing our perceptions is hard and difficult when you have looked at something the same way for a long time, but the view must change and start seeing as Jesus sees. We must have a vision that reflects the vision of Christ for our church and for our communities.

Reflection Questions

1. What is the view and perception that you have for your church? Is your perception of your church healthy?
2. What are some of the steps that you can take to help you and your church to see itself in a correct God perspective?
3. Are there things that need to be stopped so that your perspective can be corrected?

Best Practices/Ideas

1. Start thinking, talking, and walking as a church that has high self-esteem. Walking in the truth that you are worthy and valuable where God has placed you.

2. Stop thinking about your church as being small or ineffective and start seeing your church the way God sees your church with every message and every class that is taught.

3. Take the necessary steps to help your people and your leadership to have a healthy perspective on your church and its ministries.

4. Minister in your neighborhood in such a way that you and the church are the best neighbors they have. Your church is essential, so work knowing that in everything your church does.

CHAPTER 4

Recognizing the Need for Revitalization

"Examine yourselves as to whether you are in the faith. Test
yourselves. Do you not know yourselves, that Jesus Christ
is in you? —unless indeed you are disqualified."
(2 Corinthians 13:5)

In the church I came to pastor, the need to revitalize was a conclusion the leadership had figured out for themselves. The only thing they did not know was how, when, or if it would ever happen. I was very fortunate; I did not have to deal with much resistance to change. Yes, there were still some rough moments I had to deal with. Some wanted to dig their heels in and push back against change but it could have been a lot worse. Even the ones that resisted knew they needed to do something, but they did not expect how much had to change in order to get the church back on the right track.

What we had to do was heal all the sick church ailments that plagued the church and make it healthy again. That took lots of teaching about healthy church habits, preaching about a healthy lifestyle, mentoring healthy mindsets, and setting healthy examples for us to see and live.

Our denomination had published material and it was made available about the time we started the revitalization journey; it was perfect timing, to publish "Nazarene Essentials." It talked about who we are as Nazarenes and walked us through the Articles of Faith and items that are distinct to the Church. That study of lessons that we walked through, helped us identify who and what we were and what we believed. That started us on the right track and gave people more confidence in our church and our beliefs. Make real moves to revitalize your church and God will move in your congregation and help you and the body to be a healthy and thriving church.

Probably the hardest thing for us to do is to look at ourselves and examine and recognize that we need help. That is one of the toughest things to admit. The same goes for the churches that we serve. Come on guys and gals we know it is true…we have at one time or another, looked at ourselves in the mirror and we have sucked in the tummy that has started sliding over the belt or combed a little more hair over that thinning spot on our head. It is natural for us to want to look better than what we do. It is no different for churches.

For real revitalization to happen we must really take a serious look at ourselves. We must stop sucking in the gut and take an honest look at who we are.

Church Revitalization starts by seeing what is around us.

Do you ever think of the people that once had a vision for Christ's work on that very spot where the church sits? At a point in time, God spoke to someone's heart about planting a church. Probably through much prayer, that person was reassured that God called them to start that church, so they set forth-telling others of the plan. That person started looking for locations to meet. Some start in houses, others in a storefront, and others in borrowed churches. Then the day came, and the location was found. An empty piece of property would become the home, the location where your church now sits. The ground was broken, and the construction started, now stands your church. Can you picture all the sacrifice and hard work that got them that far? Do you sense the passion that must have rung out through the building at one time? Can you imagine the celebration and enthusiasm that must have existed in that first service? Can you hear the testimonies of salvation and sanctification that must have been experienced here? Or do you only see neglect and abandonment? Do you see anything at all?

Traveling on country backroads, you see many sights and many times you see a church that is old and dilapidated. What are the first thoughts that go through your mind as you see these places? Maybe the sign has not been changed in months or even years. The grass and weeds are taking over the once gravel parking lot. Possibly the church hasn't seen a coat of paint in a generation.

As you drive through the countryside you see places that are picturesque and scenic, but in other parts of the community, you may catch a glimpse of an old broken-down house with laundry on the line. There might be an old car in the driveway, what do you think about the people that live there? Is it just another place that we passed by?

Church revitalization starts by seeing what is around us. It is looking at our community and seeing the needs that are not being met. It is seeing the people that are lost and in need of a savior. It is seeing the brokenness and the pain. It is seeing that there is more that we can do to reach those around us. We start by seeing the vision that God has placed on our hearts. We start by seeing what He is calling us to do. We start by stepping out in faith and obedience. We start by taking risks for the kingdom. We start by being obedient to what God has called us to do. When we see the needs around us, we can't help but be moved to action. We can't help but want to do something to make a difference. That is how church revitalization starts - seeing what is around us and being moved to action. It is about seeing the vision that God has for our community and taking the steps necessary to fulfill it. It is about seeing the needs of those in our communities and doing all that we can to help meet them. It is about seeing beyond ourselves and seeing God's plan for this world, working together with Him to bring His kingdom here on earth. Let us be people who are moved by what we see, who are willing to take risks for the sake of Christ, and who seek to do all that we can in order to further His mission in this world. Let us start seeing church revitalization today, starting with seeing what is around us and moving forward with the vision that God has placed in our hearts.

How do we see the church that you attend?

What do you see when you drive by a boarded-up church? Many times, we become so familiar with our surroundings that we are blind to the community around us. Do you see a church that died because it was stuck in tradition or legalism? Do you become sad, knowing that it represents a light on a hill that has become darkened? When you pass a small church on the side street of a small town, do you see a vital part of the faith community providing a witness of the Gospel? Or do you see a church draining resources and should be closed so that the resources could be utilized better elsewhere?[1] Small rural churches are vital to the work of the Kingdom. Over seven in ten churches have less than 100 in attendance on any given Sunday. They are small and often neglected. How do you see the church you lead? Do you see a congregation that is getting older and smaller in size without any new families coming in? Do you see a church that holds its breath each Sunday when the offering is taken to see if you have enough to keep the lights on? Do you see a church that is just hanging on by the last thread? It is how we see and respond to these questions which dictates your actions in your church. If you see your church as dying and hopeless then chances are your church is not likely to ever turn around to be anything other than what it is now. If our thoughts and our actions are always a reaction to despair, gloom, and desperation, then our actions are directed to that rather than to life-giving ministry.

How do you see the community that you live in?

Some see rural America as a place to retreat from the noise and the confusion of urban life. It's a place to relax and enjoy recreational activities. Others see rural America as a decaying and dying landscape where people are stuck in the past and are as rundown as the old homes and churches that dot the landscape. Still, others see rural people as closed-minded bigots who reject modern society and perpetuate longstanding racial and economic biases. We can become so familiar and comfortable with our surroundings, that we become blind to the very community that we live in.

What do you see? Christ sees people who are without a Shepherd. To Him, these communities represent individuals who have been devastated by the ravaging effects of sin and are in desperate need of the Gospel. Too often, when driving through the countryside of rural communities, we fail to see this.

"Rural America is rapidly becoming a spiritual wasteland, where churches are being closed because they are overlooked and cast aside by the larger church community as a place deemed too insignificant or unworthy of our attention.[1]" Rural areas are quickly becoming the new ghetto, with persistent poverty, drug use among young people, and crime, all of which are becoming widespread problems. We also see incredibly long-standing and increased racial tension. When we see the true spiritual condition of rural America, we simply cannot ignore it. We need to ask "Why?" And "What would Christ have us to do to help?" To see with the eyes of Christ is to see rural people who are "distressed and dispirited like sheep without a Shepherd" (Matthew 9:36).

How do we see ourselves in ministry opportunities?

When we see the true spiritual condition of rural America, we simply cannot ignore it. We need to ask why? What role does the church, that I lead play in this? What would Christ have us do to help? To see with the eyes of Christ is to see all who are "Distressed and dispirited like sheep without a Shepherd" (Matthew 9:36). But before you can see what is around you, you must first recognize who you are as a church in Christ and in the community that you are living in.

Being the Church that God Intends for us to be.

> *"Therefore I also, after I heard of your faith in the Lord Jesus and your love for all the saints, do not cease to give thanks for you, making mention of you in my prayers: that the God of our Lord Jesus Christ, the Father of glory, may give to*

you the spirit of wisdom and revelation in the knowledge of Him, the eyes of your understanding being enlightened; that you may know what is the hope of His calling, what are the riches of the glory of His inheritance in the saints, and what is the exceeding greatness of His power toward us who believe, according to the working of His mighty power which He worked in Christ when He raised Him from the dead and seated Him at His right hand in the heavenly places, far above all principality and power and might and dominion, and every name that is named, not only in this age but also in that which is to come.

And He put all things under His feet, and gave Him to be head over all things to the church, which is His body, the fullness of Him who fills all in all" (Eph. 1:15-23)

Paul is talking to a church that has it all...but is living as if they have nothing. They have everything going for them but are short-sighted on the potential they possess. Paul wrote to them to encourage them to walk in the light of Christ and to draw upon the marvelous riches that were available to them through Christ. He wanted them to draw from the spiritual bank account that they had access to and all rights to Adoption, Acceptance, Redemption, Forgiveness, Wisdom, Inheritance, The seal of the Holy Spirit, Life, Grace, and Citizenship. In short, every spiritual blessing is needed for living a full life in Christ in this world.

This letter to the Ephesians is more than a way of life for individuals, but for the church also. The question could be asked, where does our hope lie? What is our source and our provision for living the Christian life? The foundation of the Church has been and will continue to be built with Christ as the cornerstone. Everything is measured by and built upon and trusted in this Stone.

This is a tremendous foundation in terms of the believer's position, understanding who we are in Christ, and understanding the greatness of our resources in Christ. This prayer in Ephesians 1 is a prayer that God would enable the believer to see and understand the resources that are available in Christ, and not only the individual, but the Church as a whole. That is a basic and fundamental reality, but it is lost to so many people and churches today. I don't think many people understood what it really is to be fully in Christ and Christ fully in you. If we really understand, then we would be nurturing and cultivating our relationship with Him even more closely. We would be pulling ourselves up close, and looking for any opportunity to be in the presence of God.

The problem the Ephesus church had in Revelation 2 is the same problem that many churches today are experiencing decline and slow death because they no longer possess that "first love." Say that to a congregation and I guarantee you the response would be a swift and firm "Not us!" But the sad reality for so many is denial of their coldness and lack of God's Spirit in their services or devotional time. Where has the fire gone? My mind's eye sees images of those drifting away, distancing from the pain, and loss. Relationships weaken with time and distance, and it is no different in our relationship with the Lord.

In Ephesians 1:15-23, the letter lends itself to the fact that the Ephesians were not living up to the fullness that God provided. They were living as if being a follower of Christ was not enough for salvation. That there was more of Christ that had to be obtained and struggled for. That you had to do "this to" get it all. They also were hanging on to old ways, the old life.

It is a direct result of the text that we are not to live in a way that is beneath what God has called us to. To come to an understanding of what it means to be filled with the Holy Spirit, one must first understand the Greek word pleroo. This word is found in other places in Scripture and can be translated as to make full, to fill up, or to be completed. When used in the context of the filling of the Holy Spirit, it is best translated as to be controlled by. To be controlled by the Holy Spirit is to allow Him to lead and guide our lives according to His will and not our own.

The need for more comes not from God to you but from you to God. We received all that God had to offer when we accepted Jesus as our Savior and when the blood was applied to our sins. Our spiritual bank was filled up at that point. God bankrupt Heaven to deposit in your account. Paul talks about the importance and command to walk in the Spirit of God.

"There is therefore now no condemnation to those who are in Christ Jesus, who do not walk according to the flesh, but according to the Spirit. For the law of the Spirit of life in Christ Jesus has made me free from the law of sin and death. For what the law could not do in that it was weak through the flesh, God did by sending His own Son in the likeness of sinful flesh, on account of sin: He condemned sin in the flesh, that the righteous requirement of the law might be fulfilled in us who do not walk according to the flesh but according to the Spirit. For those who live according to the flesh set their minds on the things of the flesh, but those who live according to the Spirit, the things of the Spirit" *(Romans 8:1-5)*

The main point in Ephesians is the concept and term "in Christ." It is "in Christ" that we as individuals and especially the church become and are transformed into the image of Christ and heirs of God. In chapter 1 Paul writes that we are chosen by the Father (1:3-6), redeemed by the Son (1:7-12), and sealed by the Spirit (1:13-14).

Paul knew the importance of walking in the hope, riches, and the power of God. That is why he prayed this first prayer. This prayer was prayed with precision and with purpose. (Vs 15-18a) That we comprehend our hope, (Vs. 18b) That we comprehend our riches, (Vs. 19-21) That we comprehend His power, (Vs. 22-23) That we comprehend our responsibility.

The weight or emphasis of the prayer is that we, as the church, would live out loud as a body of Christ in our communities and homes. That we would live it out in front of everyone that sees and encounters us. That we would live the life of Christ to the world around us. In a way that people would think and say, "there is something different about that church and its people." That our lights would shine in such a way that is unmistakable to others.

"Jesus is head over all things to the church, which is His body, being His eyes, ears, hands, feet and especially His heart. We are the fullness of Him. Which is His completeness, attributes, character, and likeness. Jesus is the One who fulfills us, everything He is, His presence, His compassion, His heart. We are the reflection of Him.

A Christian must be a sign of contradiction in the world. A Christian is one who his entire life chooses between good and evil, lies and truth, love and hate, God and Satan…Today more than ever there is a need for our light to shine, so that through us, through our deeds, through our choices, people can see the Father who is in Heaven. The holiest moment of the church service is the moment when God's people, strengthened by the preaching and sacraments, go out of the church door into the world to be the Church. We don't go to church; we are the Church.

We must recognize who we are as a church and anything different than what God says we are is missing the mark. If this is the case, then we are in need of revitalization and renewal. Small churches, rural churches: Be all you can be in Christ!

1. **Small churches must believe that they can be everything God intends for them to be.** Small churches can be vibrant, active participants in the work God is doing in the world. We want to do better. We can do better. We will do better. But we can't do it alone. Small and rural churches need to see that they are not the forgotten stepchild. They are not secondary to the body of Christ. They are not just some afterthought of denominational leaders. The physical size of their congregation does not disqualify them or make them any less significant for the Kingdom work that God has for them in the community they reside.

2. **Small churches need to understand what purpose God has for them**. Small and rural churches play an important role in the Kingdom. You don't see mega-churches on the country roads 30 minutes or further from the interstate. You don't see lots of outreach money pouring into sparsely populated counties. God has a specific purpose and plan for each small rural church that is dotted across this vast country that we live in. If you would count the total number of people that go to mega-churches versus the total number of people going to the countless numbers of small churches, the majority go to these small and rural churches. There

is power in the small number of people that go to your church. The big churches can't do in your community, what you can do, and that is through the power of your presence. Your presence and your boots on the ground make all the difference. But for that power and presence to happen you must recognize and decide to get out and into the community and build those relationships. That is the purpose that you have, to make relationships. We were created by God, for God, in the image of God to have a relationship with Him first, but to have a relationship with each other also. That is the purpose God has for you.

3. **Small churches need to be unapologetic in obedience.** The reason many churches need revitalization is that somewhere along the way they quit being obedient in all things. That seems like a harsh and rude statement, but it is the truth. Obedience has slacked somewhere in the church's life and as a result, the church has turned its attention to itself. It has become less and less concerned with those outside of the walls. To have true revitalization, we must recognize the need for obedience regardless of the cost. Obedience is the only true measure of serving God to a point of absolute abandonment to His service.

Many people think that small churches have problems, and usually list the causes of those problems as:

- Church-centric - focused on themselves
- threatened by change
- filled with division and fighting with each other
- have no concern for their communities and neighbors
- poor leadership and management
- settling for status-quo and for less.

These are not accurate descriptions of a small church; it is the accurate description of an unhealthy church. The problems most people see as being the inherent problems in small churches aren't about size or their "smallness," it's about their sickness, and sickness can happen in churches of any size.

Telling Our Story

Everyone has probably heard the story of the man that was caught in a great flood that forced him to climb out on his roof to escape the rising waters. A fellow was stuck on his rooftop in a flood. He was praying to God for help. Soon a man in a rowboat came by and the fellow shouted to the man on the roof, "Jump in, I can save you." The stranded fellow shouted back, "No, it's OK, I'm praying to God, and he is going to save me." So, the rowboat went on. Then a motorboat came by. "The fellow in the motorboat shouted, "Jump in, I can save you." To this the stranded man said, "No thanks, I'm praying to God, and he is going to save me. I have faith." So, the motorboat went on. Then a helicopter came by, and the pilot shouted down, "Grab this rope and I will lift you to safety." To this, the stranded man again replied, "No thanks, I'm praying to God and he is going to save me. I have faith." So, the helicopter reluctantly flew away. Soon the water rose above the rooftop and the man drowned. He went to Heaven and finally got his chance to discuss this whole situation with God, at which point he exclaimed, "I had faith in You, but you didn't save me, you let me drown. I don't understand why!" To this God told them he sent a rowboat, and a helicopter. What more did he expect?

Too often this is the same scenario for our struggling churches across America. The strange thing is as churches become more in need of help the more that they tend to retreat into themselves rather than calling out for help. Fortunately for the church, I pastor, they saw that they needed help and needed it quickly. They reached out to the superintendent and started the process of looking for someone they hoped could help them.

Not all churches are as fortunate. I know of one that recently closed because although they prayed for God to help them to grow and be vibrant again, they were like the man on the roof. When the opportunity came to help them, they did not take the steps needed for revitalization. It was not something that happened overnight, they sat on their roof for decades.

Reflection Questions

1. Has your church been willing to open its eyes and see what is around them? What is it that you see?
2. Is your church in need of revitalization? What are the first steps that you need to take?
3. Do you believe God has a specific purpose for your church? What is it? Explain it out loud.
4. List 3 ministry opportunities that you see in your community. What would it take to accomplish those opportunities?

Best Practices/Ideas

1. Start by doing a checkup of what level your members understand the foundations of their faith and of the church. Do they understand the Statement of Faith, and what are the core values of the church, and denomination?
2. Take leadership, church, and community assessments to determine the strongest needs in each of these areas.
3. Take an honest and thorough look at yourself and the church to identify what areas you are weakest in and address those areas.
4. Accentuate the positives and strengths of your church. Does your church have a special gifting or ability that only your church can fulfill? Use that ability to the fullest.

CHAPTER 5

Prayer is the Fuel for the Fire

When Solomon had finished praying, fire came down from heaven
and consumed the burnt offering and the sacrifices; and the glory
of the Lord filled the temple. And the priests could not enter the
house of the Lord, because the glory of the Lord had filled the Lord's
house. When all the children of Israel saw how the fire came down,
and the glory of the Lord on the temple, they bowed their faces
to the ground on the pavement, and worshiped and praised the
Lord, saying: "For He is good, For His mercy endures forever."
(2 Chronicles 7)

It didn't take long for me to see that our Wednesday night prayer meetings were less than exciting, to say the least. Wait a minute, that's an understatement! They were as dry and dead as a potted plant left in Death Valley in July. There was no power in the meetings. We found ourselves asking people to pray about everything under the sun from Aunt Molly's health issues to Uncle Bud's bunions. From one person's pet pig to another's bladder control problems. I am not making light of these issues in people's lives but out of the hour we would spend together we spent 55 minutes talking about requests and 5 minutes praying for those requests. Heaven forbid if the person praying, forgets to mention one request that we just spent 55 minutes talking about. It was agonizing from start to finish. I admit I found myself at the end of the meetings breathing a sigh of relief it was over each Wednesday night. I remember thinking there must be more. Something had to change

The major change happened in our church when we intentionally and deliberately studied and practiced prayer, corporately and individually. While attending one of the first district assemblies after becoming a pastor, something significant happened to me that changed everything. Before each morning session of the assembly, the district superintendent would have a time of corporate prayer for the purpose of calling out to God to move in that day's activities. As I walked into the hall and witnessed all the people that were praying, fervently crying out to God, asking for His favor in the place, I experienced a move of The Holy Spirit in me revealing that this was what was missing. What I was witnessing was the very thing our church needed. This was the "more" that I was longing for and wanting. I realized we needed to experience and have that same hunger and thirst for His Spirit in our congregation and our meetings.

When the assembly was over, and we went home to our church, I stood up in front of the congregation and told them of the events that had happened and what God had revealed to me in those meetings. I told them that prayer was going to be the utmost important thing that we could do to help our church turn around and be revitalized. We needed to take our Wednesday night prayer meeting, and get back to the business of prayer, and not just request. Transforming it back into a prayer meeting, seeking God for help with the church, ministry, outreach and overall health of the church body. It was not long after we set our attention to deliberate and intentional prayer, we would come into the meeting at 7 PM and by 7:10 PM we were crying out to God and having prayer for the whole time, often way after 8 PM. I found if we can get serious about prayer and what it can do for us and the church, things do happen, and hearts are renewed. We begin to align ourselves with what God wants for us and not only our own requests. We start to walk along with God in perfect fellowship and communion.

Igniting the Fire

Every man has done it…thrown some highly combustible substance on a dying or struggling fire to try to accelerate the whole process. The possibility of becoming a flaming marshmallow that is frantically extinguished is a very real reality, or the most common result, having scorched eyebrows and a singed ego. Although at times we try to take things dangerously into our own hands, the fire of God must come from God. Prayer is the key to what God has for us as a people and a church body. God has a beautiful plan for every one of us in our church. Prayer is the fuel for that fire.

Very few of the billions of people on this planet will ever maximize the full potential that God has placed inside them. Most people live mediocre lives. The full extent of their capabilities and talents goes untapped. Many are not even aware of the tremendous potential they possess.

What is "potential"?

Potential is your unused strengths, hidden talents, untapped abilities, and capped or locked up capabilities. There is a great wealth of potential within you. Potential can be characterized by a stick of dynamite. It is an object that has great capabilities bound inside it. Capabilities of great destruction or construction depending on the use. All that potential and power can be released by a single spark. You must decide if you will deprive or bless the world with those gifts that are locked away inside you. If you decide you do want to have that potential released, then the next step will be to understand the principles God has established for unlocking that potential.

Keys to unlocking potential:

1. **Everything starts with prayer.** Simply stated, prayer is talking with God. We pray when we open our hearts to the Almighty. As simple as this is, it is also something people need to hear.

Too many people feel that prayer is a certain word spoken VERY loudly. Others feel prayer is something that takes place in a certain place or with a certain posture. But none of those things are requirements for true prayer. In fact, you can sound holy and not be doing anything other than talking to yourself or the ceiling. True prayer is open, honest, humble, and personal. It is a matter of relationship, and it can happen no other way.

2. **Create a culture or lifestyle of prayer.** The conversation is a part of any vital and growing relationship. We sometimes measure the quality of a marriage relationship by how well the couple communicates. To state it another way, one of the first things people point to as evidence that a marriage is in trouble is a lack of communication. If you do not have a desire to communicate, then you do not have a desire for a meaningful relationship. The same is true for our relationship with the Father. The true, honest, heartfelt conversation is a sign of a healthy relationship. A lack of conversation or conversation only in public is a sign of a relationship in trouble. It is through the prayer life of a committed, devoted servant that God can bring out the strength and power He wants to demonstrate in the child of God.

3. **Listening is part of prayer.** Paul commands us to pray always. 1 Thessalonians 5:17 says to "pray without ceasing." Obviously, it cannot mean we are to be in a head-bowed, eyes-closed posture all day long. Paul is not referring to non-stop talking, but rather an attitude of God-consciousness and God-surrender that we carry with us all the time. Every waking moment is to be lived in an awareness that God is with us and that He is actively involved and engaged in our thoughts and actions. The Greek reads, "Pray without intermission"; without allowing prayerless gaps to intervene between the times of prayer. When we are in a state of continual conscious prayer, we can then hear God respond and speak to us so we can know and hear His heart. If prayer is to be a conversation with the Almighty then we must allow time for God to speak to us. Otherwise, we are giving a lecture to God, informing Him of everything we have already decided needs

to be done and prayer is more information for God rather than guidance from God. In fact, it is far more important what God says to you than what you say to God.

4. **Repentance is essential for effective prayer.** Prayer changes us. Prayer doesn't change God, it doesn't change things, nor does it change circumstances. Prayer changes us. Our prayers often reflect this statement, "Everyone thinks of changing humanity, but no one thinks of changing themselves." Real prayer changes us. Repentance is the turning from our ways to God's ways.

   Real prayer is not only soul-satisfying; it is life-changing. When you and I spend time with Jesus, He changes us. To pray is to change. Prayer is the central avenue God uses to transform us. If we are unwilling to change, we will abandon prayer as a noticeable characteristic of our lives. The closer we come to the heartbeat of God, the more we see our own needs, and the more we desire to be conformed to Christ. The transformation that Christ provides is more of a "turn-formation", turning from our evil ways. Don't pray unless you want to change. Prayer propels us into action. Prayer advances God's Kingdom. Prayer ignites a church to move outside its walls.

5. **Obeying the voice that comes through prayer.** Prayer unleashes the power of God. Two characteristics dominated the apostle's prayer meetings: God's presence and God's power. Is it any wonder that the evil one seeks valiantly to keep Christ-followers from praying? When we don't pray Satan has won the battle. But when we do pray, the presence and the power of God are unleashed. For those disciples in Jerusalem, they experienced the power of God in a very tangible and real way. "When they had prayed, the place where they were assembled was shaken" (Acts 4:31).

The practice of prayer in a believer's life is an incredible, virtually untapped power source. Prayer moves the hand of God. Prayer prevails. Prayer turns ordinary mortals into men and women of power with the enormous potential that God has placed in them at their disposal. It is the key that unlocks the storehouse of God's riches. Prayer is the call that moves Heaven to act on behalf of the earth. Seek after the potential God has placed in us through intentional, purposeful prayer!

You must establish a relationship with God — the source of your potential. You must understand how God made you to function: by faith and by love. You must know your purpose in life (your potential was given for just that). You must identify the resources that help unlock your potential. You must know, find, or create the right environment needed to function at your peak performance level. Part of this is daily contact with God. You must realize that potential is expressed through hard work and persistence. You must cultivate your potential. Fertilize it like a seed. You must guard your potential — from laziness, distractions, and compromise. Your potential is God's gift to you. He expects you to use it! That key, talent, power, and potential is released through fervent prayer.

The Importance of Prayer

Paul was a man of prayer and Paul knew the importance of prayer in his life and in others. *"For God is my witness, whom I serve with my spirit in the gospel of his Son, that without ceasing I make mention of you always in my prayers." (Romans 1:9).* He prayed "without ceasing" for the Roman Christians. To the Corinthian church, he wrote: *"I thank my God always on your behalf."* To the Ephesians: *"[I] cease not to give thanks for you, making mention of you in my prayers".* To Philippi: *"Always in every prayer of mine for you all making requests with joy".* And to the Colossians: *"For this cause we also, since the day we heard it, do not cease to pray for you". "We give thanks to God always for you all, making mention of you in our prayers".*

He also prayed constantly for his personal disciples.

Timothy and Philemon. *"Without ceasing I have remembrance of thee in my prayers night and day". "I thank my God, making mention of thee always in my prayers".*

Paul also preached what he practiced.

"Pray without ceasing," "In everything give thanks". "Continuing instant in prayer". "Continue in prayer and watch in the same with thanksgiving". "Giving thanks always for all things." Paul learned this intensity of prayer from the Master himself, Jesus, *"Very early in the morning, while it was still dark, he got up, went out, and made his way to a deserted place. And he was praying there" (Mark 1:35).* It was common knowledge among the disciples that they would find Jesus praying during the early morning hours. Jesus knew the importance of getting alone in prayer. And the disciples knew if they needed Him, they would have to go into the place where Jesus would retreat for prayer. On the very night that he betrayed him, Judas knew exactly where to go to find Jesus which was His place of prayer in the garden.

Every time the Lord Jesus faced an important decision, He prayed. When He was being tempted to do things by the world's methods instead of by the Fathers, He prayed. When it was time to choose His disciples, He prayed the entire night. If Jesus thought it was important enough that it required a whole night of prayer in order to determine the Father's mind, how long might it take us in prayer to clearly determine our Father's will for our lives and for our church's direction?

Jesus was so often surrounded by people demanding His time, requesting miracles from Him. He would retreat to deserted, lonely places to hear the Father's voice without distraction. Many times, Jesus had people that were trying to dictate the direction that He should be going. The disciples wanted Jesus to go where more people were so that He would gain more followers. The crowds also wanted to make Him their King. However, Satan tempted Jesus to make a few compromises along the way in order to grow His following even larger. Although Jesus knew that crowds would flock to Him, His mission was to obey His Father. Just as Jesus led by example, we too often get distracted from what God wants us to do when leading our congregations. It is important for us to remember that we need quiet and stillness so we can hear God's voice speaking to us.

It was prayer that set the agenda for Jesus' ministry. And prayer should be the compass for our leadership of the church. Prayer came before the miracles, prayer brought Him encouragement at crucial moments, prayer enabled Him to go to the cross, and prayer kept Him there despite excruciating pain. You may have been through times of struggle and surely times of uncertainty, but Jesus can be our example going forward and beyond. Follow the Savior's example and let your time alone with God, in prayer, set the agenda for your life and for your ministry.

What is Prayer?

The simple answer is this: prayer is talking with God. It is the communication of the human soul with the Lord who created that soul. Prayer is the primary way for the believer in Jesus Christ to communicate his emotions and desires with God and to have fellowship with God. "Christian prayer in its full New Testament meaning is prayer addressed to God as Father, in the name of Christ as Mediator, and through the enabling grace of the indwelling Spirit."[1]

Prayer is described in the Bible as seeking God's favor (Exodus 32:11), pouring out one's soul to the Lord (1 Samuel 1:15), crying out to heaven (2 Chronicles 32:20), drawing near to God (Psalm 73:28, KJV), and kneeling before the Father (Ephesians 3:14). Paul wrote, *"Do not be anxious about anything, but in every situation, by prayer and petition, with thanksgiving, present your requests to God. And the peace of God, which transcends all understanding, will guard your hearts and your minds in Christ Jesus"* *(Philippians 4:6–7).* Worry about nothing; pray about everything. Prayer is the wonderful privilege of the created having communion with the Creator. It is through prayer that we receive all the help that we need to sustain and provide for ourselves in the journey of life.[2]

Reasons for Prayer

There are several good reasons to pray. It is a great privilege. Can you think of any greater honor than to have an audience with the One who rules over ALL creation? To think that the One that spoke everything into being would desire to speak with us is enough to set your head into a spin. We have been invited to talk with the One who put the stars in place. We are invited to seek counsel from the One who is truth and wisdom. We are invited to sit down with the One who knows all things. The One that knows us inside and out. We have the opportunity to express ourselves to the very One that put breath in our lungs.

We should also pray because we are in a fierce battle. Constantly we are warned of the devil's intention to neutralize and demoralize us. We are told that *"our struggle is not against flesh and blood, but against the rulers, against the authorities, against the powers of this dark world and against the spiritual forces of evil in the heavenly realms." (Eph. 6:10).* We are in a battle, and we need the help of God. The enemy has marshaled his armies. . .when we neglect prayer, we go into battle unarmed. Weakness is not of God; it is of the flesh. Prayer arms us and strengthens us. Do you find it at all helpful to know that Jesus, the incarnate Son of God, found it necessary to pray in the garden before He faced the cross and Calvary? If He did not feel He could face the battle on His own strength. Neither should we.

Prayer is a strong deterrent to sin in our lives. In the quiet times of private honest prayer, God exposes the rationalizations and the excuses that we use to cater to sin. In prayer God holds a mirror up to our lives so we can see the way we really are. . .and repent. Our potential will NOT be realized with sin in our life, hindering and crippling the possibilities God has in store for us to do with Him. And finally, prayer makes a difference. I can't tell you how it "works" . . . but I know that circumstances change when people pray. Diseases can be healed, strength is imparted, guidance is given, hearts are softened, and needs are met. I know when I pray for others it helps them. I also know when I pray, I am changed and helped as well. My potential is released and manifests in and through my obedient prayer.

It is no secret that any church that experiences revitalization first focused on prayer. In every case without exception, the pastor and leadership of that particular church had leaders that believed that prayer changes things and it matters for the absolute health of the church. When a church, pastor, and leaders really believe that prayer makes a difference, they'll make prayer a priority in their own lives and in the church's life also.

Revitalization cannot go any further than our limited human efforts until making prayer the highest priority in your church. The New Testament church serves as the model of a church that prays. Stories of churches that grow as they prayed will encourage you as you strive to become a church "devoted...to prayer" (Acts 2:42). Have you ever thought about how much the early church prayed? Look at these revealing clues from the book of Acts:

- 1:14 – "They all joined together constantly in prayer."
- 3:1 – "Peter and John were going up to the temple at the time of prayer."
- 4:31 – "After they prayed, the place where they were meeting was shaken."
- 6:4 – "And we will give our attention to prayer and the ministry of the word."
- 10:9 – "Peter went up on the roof to pray."
- 12:5 – "The church was earnestly praying to God for him."
- 13:3 – "After they had fasted and prayed, they placed their hands on them and sent them off."
- 14:23 – "Paul and Barnabas...with prayer and fasting, committed them to the Lord."
- 16:25 – "Paul and Silas were praying and singing hymns to God."
- 20:36 – "When Paul had said this, he knelt down with all of them and prayed."
- 28:8 – "Paul went in to see him and, after prayer, placed his hands on him and healed him."

It is clear, through scripture, that the early church was a praying church. Why? It was because they loved Jesus with all their heart, they were dependent upon God completely, and they knew that prayer made every difference in the church and in their lives.[3]

Although the early disciples needed to have direction on how to pray, talking with God was as natural for them as a wife talking to her husband or a son talking to his father. Jesus said love for them motivated Him to teach them to pray, and their love for Him motivated them to follow Him in prayer.

However, we sometimes get so busy doing church that we neglect our love relationship with God. Our church activities continue but we give too little attention to our personal spiritual walk and end up neglecting the health of the church. Driven by duty rather than by the love of God, we work harder in church but often pray less. A church that wants to be a prayer-driven church will first make sure that she has kept her first love, that is, that her members love God more than they ever had before (Revelation 2:4). If they really love Jesus, they will keep His commandments (John 14:15)[4]. The love for Jesus will be as a fire in their interbeing, burning in them like the men on the road to Emmaus (Luke 34:13-32).

Genuine prayer demonstrates not only sincere love but also absolute dependence. The prayers of the early believers showed they were dependent on God for food, health, power, protection, and guidance. They also knew that only God could grow the church (1 Corinthians 3:6-7). Our revitalization efforts must be powered by God through prayer because we are totally dependent upon His power and strength. Prayer-driven churches are churches that depend on God totally. On the other hand, churches that operate in their own power usually don't pray very much at all.[5]

The early church knew without a shadow of a doubt that prayer makes the difference. The early believers knew of the extraordinary circumstances that scripture teaches when their fathers had overcome adversity and unimaginable circumstances because of prayer. They knew the stories about Abraham praying before sacrificing his son Isaac. About Moses praying for water, and God providing it from a rock. Hannah prays for a son, whom God gave her. Solomon gained wisdom through prayer. Nehemiah sought his king's favor through prayer, and God granted that favor. Daniel's commitment to prayer landed him in the lion's den, but God protected him in the midst of the lions.

Try putting yourself in the place of the typical member of the early church. It is very likely that you would have learned the same stories they had and how effective prayer was in the Old Testament. Or maybe you had seen Jesus Himself pray and knew that His prayers were powerful. The early church members prayed knowing God still answers prayers, and they knew that *"the prayer of a righteous man is powerful and effective"* (James 5:16). Is it any wonder that the members of the early church prayed as much as they did? When we really believe that prayer makes a difference, we'll pray more with sincerity and clarity.[6]

So where do you begin to fuel the fire if you want to grow a prayer-driven revitalized church? You come to realize that praying churches have praying pastors. Praying churches have praying leaders. Praying churches make prayer a priority. Above all, prayer-driven revitalized churches believe prayer matters. They know that the fire must first be burning for God Himself and that the fire is a reflection of a relationship with Him. They pray because they love Jesus. They recognize their dependence upon God, knowing that Jesus is the head of the church (Ephesians 5:23-24). And they know from the Bible and from their own experiences that prayer really does make a difference and is the spark that ignites everything else.

To begin leading your church to be a prayer-driven revitalized church, ask God to teach you and your leadership to pray and for that desire to pray to grow more and more as you use it.

Telling our story

After that district assembly, prayer went from being a drag on our emotions to the power that ignites us as a church. I came back from that district assembly and shared with my congregation the experience I had there, and what I felt God was speaking to me. I was very honest with them about the status of our prayer life in our church. I was honest that there was no power, no conviction, and no presence in the prayers that existed in our church. The astounding thing to me after I finished speaking, was most everyone agreed with me. How could this be, all this time we have been suffering through this prayer life and no one seemed to say anything about it. It was as if everyone was suffering through it without anyone willing to speak up and say anything about it.

From that time on our prayer meetings changed. We came into the meetings and prayer with intentionality and purpose. We came into prayer meetings for a reason. We came in knowing that we had to get serious with God and open our hearts, our mouths, and our spirits so that God could speak to us in a way that we could hear and understand what he was saying to us. It was from that point on that our church's prayer life changed. We got to the point where we looked forward to the prayer meeting, which was the opposite of the case beforehand. It had become real for our church. We were no longer going through the motions doing what we thought we were supposed to be doing. The Spirit of the Lord moved mightily throughout our services.

The Holy Spirit wants to move through your services and the prayer time in your church as well. The Father knows what he wants for your church, but we must be in prayer seeking after His will and His way for us. He will reveal it to us in a powerful way. Go to your church, talk to them, and tell them that what they need is an intentional and purposeful communication with God through prayer. Come to God with no hidden agenda and no request in our hands to seek from Him. We must be willing to come to God and seek after Him for who He is, and not for what He can give us.

Reflection Questions

1. Evaluate the overall spiritual condition of your church. What can you do as a leader and a pastor to improve your church's prayer life?
2. What can be done to address any weaknesses in your church or leadership?
3. Becoming a praying church usually requires significant change. What do you think will be required in order to become a praying church? What will be required of you?
4. Pray that all church leaders and members, beginning with you, will capture the vision of being a praying church.

Best Practices/Ideas

1. Pastor and leaders, you must set the example of prayer and its importance to the whole church.

2. Have an extended time of study and lessons on practices of prayer, so all can learn to pray.

3. Have services that are devoted to prayer. Cry out to God for the church and the ministry.

4. Prayer walking your neighborhood is a great way to meet neighbors and introduce yourself.

5. Utilizing the apps that available online for resourcing and finding out who your neighbors are such as "Bless every home."

6. There are low-cost services that can send out specialized postcards to all people that move into your area inviting and telling about your church.

CHAPTER 6

Receiving the Vision

I was not disobedient unto the heavenly vision (Acts 26:19).

"In his heart a man plans his course, but the Lord determines his steps." (Proverbs 16:9).

It doesn't matter if you are writing a book like this, preparing a paper for a class assignment, or starring at a blank canvas, the question remains the same. Where do I start?

When I came to interview before the church board there was a lot of conversation about what they were looking for in a pastor for their church. Most of the conversation was directed by the District Superintendent because the leadership team really did not know what to ask. They knew they wanted families to come in, and they knew they wanted to see children's programing grow in the church but past that, they had no idea what to ask or to discuss.

It did not take long to understand the situation in this church. They were desperate for a solution to help them resolve this death spiral they were experiencing. Once they were done with their questions, I in turn started asking them questions. The first question I asked them was, "Who do you say you are?" Followed by, "who would the community say you are?" With eyes looking at me and mouths gaped open, all I got was awkward silence. They had no clue how to answer those questions. This is the problem for most churches today in America, they have no idea how to define themselves other than "we are a close family." That's OK but your defining characteristics should be more in depth than that.

Many churches today are running the course without knowing which way they are running. Truthfully, if they would just look down, they would see that they are on a treadmill going nowhere fast. What most churches lack is a clear and concise vision.

"THE NEED FOR VISION"

Any successful endeavor requires a vision...The word vision, literally means the ability to see things that are visible, but it also is used to mean the ability to see other things as well. In other aspects it can mean, "unusual competence in discernment or perception; intelligent foresight." More suitable for our application is the word visionary. Being a visionary is "the art of seeing things invisible", such ventures as these in business or politics require "men and women of vision." Companies require CEOs with vision, countries require leaders with vision. Without the ability to visualize worthy goals and how these can be realized, very little of importance is achieved. Martin Luther King and John F.Kennedy are fine examples of great visionary men with worthy visions.

Vision and mission statements define the purpose of an organization and instill a sense of belonging and identity to the ones involved in the organization. This motivates them to work harder in order to achieve success. It gives the right mindset for the venture to prosper to its fullest potential. The mission statement provides the direction that is to be followed by the organization while the vision statement provides the goal (or the destination) to be reached by following the direction. It helps to properly align the resources of an organization toward achieving a successful future. The mission statement provides the organization with a clear and effective guide for making decisions, while the vision statement ensures that all the decisions made are properly aligned with what the organization hopes to achieve. The vision and mission statements provide a focal point that helps to align everyone within the organization, thus ensuring everyone is working towards a single purpose. This helps to increase efficiency and productivity in the organization.

In the Lord's work it is no different, we desperately need an elevated vision of what it is all about . . . we need greater goals (what can be done) and greater objectives (how it can be done). But unlike the world's standard, we seek to receive our vision from the Creator Himself. We do not rely on charismatic leaders to direct us in any vision that they might have. We rely on the Father himself to give us the vision. Jesus told us that he does nothing except for what the Father shows Him. *"For the Father loves the Son and shows Him all things that He Himself does; and He will show Him greater works than these, that you may marvel" (John 5:20).* Jesus certainly had a great vision: the saving of souls! We need to have visions that are worthy of the "King of kings and Lord of lords"

What can help us to elevate and enlarge our vision in the Lord's work? Let's first notice how an inadequate vision can stifle our work...Let me give you two ways that our vision can be inadequate. Suppose a man is driven by the "vision" of "making as much money as possible. Two things may keep him from making as much money as he should. He may be limited in his idea of what is "a lot of money" and He may never make any specific plans other than have the vague notion of "making as much as possible." His problem? His vision: first, it may be too small concerning what can be done. Second, it may be too general without any plan for what he can be doing to make his vision a reality.

For an illustration, let us consider our own physical eyes. We can suffer from low vision. Low vision is vision loss that can't be corrected with glasses, contacts, or surgery. It isn't blindness because limited sight remains. Low vision can include blind spots, poor night vision and blurry sight. The most common types of low vision include:

- Loss of central vision: There is a blind spot in the center of one's vision.
- Loss of peripheral (side) vision: The inability to see anything to either side, above, or below eye level. central vision, however, remains intact.

- Night blindness: The inability to see in poorly lit areas such as theaters, as well as outside at night.
- Blurred vision: Objects both near and far appear out of focus.
- Hazy vision: The entire field of vision appears to be covered with a film or glare.

All these conditions hinder our vision.

Our vision of the Lord's work may likewise be inadequate or obscured. We may have the vision of "teaching as many people the gospel as possible." This is a noble vision on the surface, but we might be afflicted by the same shortcomings as the first fellow: First, we may think too small concerning what can be done. Second, we may think too generally about what we should be doing. Many times, in my own experiences I have found that when God gives me a vision for a task or ministry to do, it is very specific and narrow in target of what it is to accomplish.

The problem of a vision that is too general is that no dream has ever been achieved except by someone who dared to flesh it out in terms of the specifics necessary to make that dream a reality. For example, it is fine to plan to go to heaven, to serve the Lord faithfully, to do the work of evangelism, but how do we do such things? By what means do we get those results? What specific, measurable actions will take us where we want to be? How much time, effort, and money will it take? We need to see our vision of the Lord's work in concrete terms of things we can do . . . and plan specifically how much of them we are going to do! If we are patient for the full answer God will reveal the whole vision to us. Yes, there are details that God allows and wants us to figure out, but He will equip and prepare us for the task at hand and give us everything we need to accomplish the mission. Parts of that vision may not be revealed right away. God may choose to reveal some as you go along, but that is fine because He will give you enough to get you going in the right direction.

The problem of a vision that is too little is when we think specifically about the Lord's work, we often fail to set our sights high enough to accomplish the full mission. There can be reasons that we do think so small. Perhaps we are hindered by our past experiences. Personal efforts made in the past may have not borne fruit and caused us to be discouraged.

Other times congregational efforts did not seem to go anywhere, and we have lost confidence in our ability to achieve the stated vision. Perhaps we have been fed a steady diet of defeatism from outside influences or from within. Told by others that people are not interested in spiritual matters anymore or telling ourselves that people are not interested. With small visions, many churches and individuals seem content with: just "keeping house for the Lord," or with just an occasional conversion, usually involving our children or spouse -- With the limited vision of many churches, little is done, and little is accomplished.

I believe the Lord intends greater things for His church, especially for those servants with a willingness to work (1Corinthians 16:8-9; Revelation 3:8). What does a vision worthy of our Lord's work require?

As you start planning your course, use everything at your disposal to determine how, when, where, and why God might use you in your current situation to be of influence for Him. Then pray earnestly, diligently, and passionately that He will direct your steps. Choose a path and pursue it, while remaining attentive to the direction the Father gives.[1] Perhaps the following thoughts might be a step in the right direction. What is it our vision needs?

The vision needs to be great.

For example, to double in attendance every year or to spread the gospel to thousands in our community each year. Now that is a "God vision"! But God will also help you through your dedicated prayer times to reveal to you how these things will happen if we don't jump too soon and allow Him to unveil the vision to its fullness. If we give Him time to unpack it for us, He will start giving you parts and pieces that will come together to show the whole plan. The amount that we can handle anyway.

Accomplishing God's vision will involve action steps in how to do it. How are we doubling in attendance every year? A fine example may be, invite two people every week to your church. By the end of the year, you will likely have at least one attending regularly. If everybody (or the majority) participates then you have doubled your attendance. This is very doable and practical for anyone to be able to do. It's a matter of being persistent, and consistent in the work of the vision, that will prevail and show the results. Another way of working toward the vision of doubling the attendance is providing transportation for people who can't drive. The question may be, is the value of a soul not worth what time or effort might be involved in picking up and driving them to service? (Matthew 16:26). If each person succeeded in just getting one person to come regularly, the attendance would easily double.

How do we spread the gospel to thousands in our community each year? A simple practice of giving a tract to one person per week. A congregation of 50 would share the gospel with more than 2500 people per year in a single church. How does that compare to the past year, was no vision present? God will reveal steps along the way if we are willing to allow Him to show us as we go along.

A vision given by God requires faith in God.

We need to have faith in the power of the gospel to save souls and produce souls that have been born again. We must have faith in the power of the Lord to open doors for His prepared servants (1Corinthians 16:8-9; Revelation 3:8), And to empower His servants wanting to do His will (Philippians 4:13). God has a work for every one of His servants He has planned since before time. The open door is the opportunity for us to walk through and into the call God the Father has for each one of us. The challenge for us all is to not only ask for doors to be open but to ask for the strength and genuine faith it will take to walk through that door once we see the opportunity in front of us.

Many of us pray for doors to open but when they finally do, we do not walk through, for whatever reason. I wonder how many of us have doors God has opened knowing we are ready, but we are unsure of that readiness within ourselves. We prayed for the doors to open but if the truth be told, we have gotten comfortable in "the room we were currently in." The room and place in which we had been for so long. Before the open door, even an empty hallway seems more secure than the unknown space into which a door may lead.

God has reasons He opens doors because He needs us on the other side. God needs us to walk through the doors. God opens doors for us for a reason, and if a door opens, we can be sure God is behind it and is on "the other side," waiting to help us. The challenge for us all is to not only ask for doors to be open but to ask for the strength and genuine faith it will take to walk through once we see the open door. God needs us on the other side. Go figure. God ...needs us...on the other side.[4]

The vision needs to be one of boldness.

Our vision needs to demonstrate boldness which is a virtue displayed often by the early Christians (Acts 4:13; 9:27; 13:46; 14:3; 19:8; 28:31) for which they prayed and solicited prayers (Acts 4:29,30; Ephesians 6:19-20). Would not everyone of us like to have spiritual boldness and courage like the early Christians? We do not have to go to expensive seminars or attend workshops so we can sharpen our skills, but we need to go to the source for the boldness and courage to fulfill the heavenly vision, and that is to the Father Himself. Ephesians 3:12 says that it is an inside work that is done, *"in whom we have boldness and access with confidence through faith in Him."*

A boldness based upon our hope in Christ (2Corinthians 3:12) and to say what needs to be said, when it needs to be said, despite the circumstances (1Thessalonians 2:2). The vision that God gives us needs to be proclaimed and carried out with all confidence and boldness that we can muster. If the message is weak then the effort will be weak, and with a weak message the vision falls short of its intended goal and purpose.

The vision needs to be one of persistence.

Not losing heart, for we shall reap in due time (Galatians 6:9). Always abounding, knowing that our labor is not in vain (1Corithians 15:58). Way too many visions are never realized because people give up too soon! There is a big difference between visionaries and dreamers. Dreamers have an idea for one minute and wonderful plans but never seem to put feet to their dreams. An effective leader spends part of everyday constantly and persistently focused on turning the vision into reality.

To do this, a leader spends time asking these questions: who are we? What is the scope of what we do? What are the things we are doing well? What are our weaknesses? What are our resources? Whom do we serve? These questions help clarify and define the vision. It is one thing to dream; it is quite another to see those dreams become reality. The effective leader spends a little bit of time every day focused on the ways to put feet to the vision.[2]

> *"Then the Lord answered me and said: "Write the vision and make it plain on tablets, that he may run who reads it. For the vision is yet for an appointed time; But at the end it will speak, and it will not lie. Though it tarries, wait for it; Because it will surely come, It will not tarry. (Habakkuk 2:2-3)*

Some of us wander from one thing to another our whole lives. We're capable of so much more, but we have never clarified our purpose in life. An out of focus purpose can't inspire us, but a crystal-clear look on God's purpose for us, rivets our attention and gives us energy to keep going until we reach our goals.

While the prophet Habakkuk was in prayer, God told him to write down the vision he was giving him. I want you to see something here, you can only hear God in the spirit when you are praying, talking, and listening in the spirit, and that spirit language is prayer.

In that day, scribes used a stylist to etch words into blocks of clay. It took work, so they thought carefully about what they wanted to write in order to avoid wasting time and tablets.

We need to write our vision down in clear, compelling language so that it grips our hearts.

A clearly written vision statement frees us from confusion so that we can run instead of wandering, stumble, or going backwards. A clear vision overcomes going with the flow and produces the inspiration to run toward our goals. But the fulfillment of our vision, God tells the Prophet, is in His

(Gods) time not ours. Seldom does anyone move in a straight line from the conception of a dream to its fulfillment. Far more often, we experience ups and downs, delays, and disappointments. These, though, won't stop us if we keep our eyes on our purpose and on the One who has given it to us.[3]

Not all vision is good. Some people have "Tunnel vision" which means that they are focusing on small and often insignificant problems or very narrow views of the vision without acting on the whole vision for the church. Tunnel vision metaphorically denotes the reluctance to consider alternatives to one's preferred line of thought; instances may include physicians treating patients, detectives considering crime suspects, or anyone predisposed to a favored outcome. Tunnel vision reduces our ability to see the whole perspective and limits our ability to make full and careful decisions. Tunnel vision takes our view off the goal or purpose for which we started in the first place. It can cause us to ramrod and plow through and not take into consideration other aspects of the vision. We can possibly be part of a God given vision for your church to reach your community by reaching out to the neighboring apartment complex that is only 2 blocks away from your church. In this outreach effort Suzy oversees a great idea to have a block party on the property of the complex. Suzy is so excited, and ideas and details are swirling in her head about all the logistics and details of the event that she starts to get so focused on her project that tunnel vision starts to close in. When we let this happen all that matters to us is the block party and all else gets pushed aside and other parts of the vision gets neglected. Instead of being present to our reality, we put the blinders on and barrel ahead towards our hopes, dreams, or in this case her mission. What Suzy forgot or neglected to see was that the children's pastor has material that she wanted to pass out and include in the block party, that there was a team of volunteers that intended on mingling and whose sole purpose is to build relationships and make connections with families and parents. But Suzy wanted everyone she could get to run booths and games. Suzy was getting tunnel vision which focused only on her project and could not see the bigger picture or the wider vision. Many times, tunnel vision is a result of fear. Fear of failing, fear of not being able to achieve perceived expectations of others, fear that you will be responsible for not coming through. Because of fear the vision and focus narrows to the point of inability to see anything else. We must remember that the vision is the Lord's and not ours. God is the One that is in control, and we are responsible to following His lead and His will. We must stay obedient to the heavenly vision as Paul says in Acts. Anais Nin, a French-Cuban-American author said, "When vision becomes tunnel vision, we do not see things as they are, we see things as we are."

It is much better to heed the words of Jesus when He said, *"Behold, I say to you, lift up your eyes and look at the fields, for they are already white for harvest!" (John 4:35).*

Telling Our Story

The people in my church may not have started off knowing who they were or where they were going, but that changed a couple years into this ministry call. Because of the uncertainty that was exhibited at the interview, I produced and passed out a church survey the second week that I pastored the church. This survey was to get a pulse of the people and see to what extent the people needed to be guided and what they understood themselves to be. The first set of questions on the short survey was asking them what they felt God wanted for our church in the next three years. I gave them 3 spaces to put their answers. The top answer was for more people to attend the church. The second response was more children.

The second set of questions that I asked had to do with "what they felt God was calling them to do in the church in the next 3 years?" There was very little response to this set of questions. This was not much of a surprise. The purpose of the surveys and the way I used them was to start the conservation, to seek the vision of God for our church.

Although the process may be long and difficult at times, it is well worth the effort put into receiving what God has for your church. Take the steps of prayer, planning, conversations, and information collection so you can be going the right direction with your church.

Reflection Questions

1. Does your church have a clear and concise vision from God for your church? If not, are you willing to start seeking one?
2. Does your church's vision include people that are outside the church walls?
3. All great visions need specific details. What is the target of your vision?

Best Practices/Ideas

1. Do a survey of some type that will gauge the church's understanding of the vision.
2. If there is a lack of knowledge for the vision, then pause and take the time to explain and affirm the vision to the people. Do not move forward till most everyone at least understands the vision.
3. Communicate the vision and then communicate it some more. Make it part of all the communication of the church.
4. The more people that are in leadership that you include in the process of developing a vision statement the more buy-in that you will get.

CHAPTER 7

Working Out the Mission from God

"Continue earnestly in prayer, being vigilant in it with thanksgiving; meanwhile praying also for us, that God would open to us a door for the word, to speak the mystery of Christ, for which I am also in chains, that I may make it manifest, as I ought to speak. Walk in wisdom toward those who are outside, redeeming the time. Let your speech always be with grace, seasoned with salt, that you may know how you ought to answer each one." (Colossians 4:2-6)

After six years, I still have the notebook that I had with all the different variations of the mission statement that I thought God was giving me to work with. After much prayer, sitting still and listening for the voice of God to direct me, I knew the direction and people that we were to minister to in our church and community.

I looked up many other church's statements, trying to come up with something out of all of them. I thought about bits and pieces from here and from there to try and formulate something. I saw many good mission statements, but none seemed to be ours. It's because they were not ours, they were someone else's. I started to think, how hard can it be to do this? I had to sit back in my office chair and quit trying to make some other church's statement fit us. They are not us, and we are not them.

As I sat in the office, I began to ask myself two questions over and over. What are we trying to do? Who are we looking to do this with? As these two questions kept running through my mind like a looped recording, I focused on each and prayed and pondered on them.

What are we trying to do?

Who are we? Where does God want to use us? What does God want us to do? What do we want this church to look like? What are we trying to do? These questions rolled through my thoughts. I needed to relax and allow God to speak to me, and that is when the process got clearer. I was trying too hard at first to come up with the answers to what we were trying to do. My thoughts went to the food ministry and then to the homeless and other people that we had met. I was trying to see the forest through the trees. I was looking too specific. I heard my spirit telling me to step back and take another look at what we were trying to do.

What were we trying to do, not just as a specific church, but as part of the bigger Kingdom of God? As I pulled further back, I was reminded that Jesus came as the Savior to restore us into a right relationship with God because sin had distorted the original image that God created us in. For God said, "Let Us make man in Our image, according to Our likeness." Man was meant to be the representation of God on earth. We were not only to resemble Him but to have His character and attributes. Sin messed all that up. Sin twisted and distorted us so much that we could no longer look like God intended.

That was it! Our work here was to help people to be restored in the image of God. To direct them to the One who ultimately came and did the work of restoration. Paul teaches that we are to take the likeness of Jesus in our life more and more each day (Romans 6:11). This is who we are, and this is what we are to do.

Who are we looking to do it with?

Now that I understood what we were trying to do, the question of who we were trying to reach became much easier. Yes, we were already serving people that needed food assistance. We were helping homeless people find housing and dignity. But again, stepping back and looking at the whole forest again, I saw a clearer picture. A picture that revealed to me that there was a common denominator, which was of brokenness and hurt in people. At first, I was looking at people that we served but I soon realized that all of us have some type of brokenness and hurt in our lives. Whether it be the homeless couple needing housing, or the family trying to feed their kids. The teenager needing guidance in life choices, or the wife dealing with a sick husband. People dealing with addiction. Broken relationships from separated couples, or the child that has not seen or talked to their parents for years. There are broken and hurting people everywhere both inside the church, and especially outside.

So, there was our mission statement, "Restoring 'the image of God' to the broken and hurting." This one line tells our whole purpose and goal. This is who we are and what we are trying to do.

Knowing what you want to say and saying it clearly is a gift. "If you don't know where you're going, any road will take you there." These are lyrics to the Beatles, George Harrison's song "Any Road." These words are as true in church leadership as in any other walk of life. Ministers must define and communicate a clear mission if the church is to be successful in fulfilling the vision that God gives a church. Vision and mission statements summarize the church's plan to fulfill the work set before them in a form that can be communicated and understood easily by the congregation.

A vision statement sets out a church's long-term objectives clearly and concisely. A vision statement is intended to inspire and motivate the church's body of believers by providing a picture of where the church is heading. It also provides a reality check for ministers and leaders, who can evaluate their efforts of ministry implementation to the fruitfulness of any ministry, in correlation to the vision statement. If a planned course of action doesn't move the church toward its vision, it may need to be revised.

A mission statement defines the direction and purpose in which a church operates and sets out its key purpose. It summarizes what the church does and why. It also outlines how the church conducts its ministries and identifies key groups to be ministered to such as addicts, homeless, hungry, or single parents and on and on. A mission statement helps congregants to understand where their contribution fits into the church's objectives. It also helps other church goers decide whether they want to be part of this congregation's mission or not. That is a sad truth but the truth just the same. Not everyone is cut out for the same thing, and there are people that will not help the cause and can even hinder it.

We must first remember that the mission starts with the Lord of the harvest. It is not the church of God that has a mission in the world, but the God of mission who has a church in the world. We need to stop starting with the church and focus instead on God's mission. Instead of existing forms of church providing the limits and shape that Christian mission should take, we need to deliver God's mission to each community and let God's mission limit and shape our churches. Mission is not something we just decide to do but it is a response to what God is already doing around us. He calls us into His work, and we are the vessels and instruments that He uses to achieve His will in that community.

Understanding the mission is the first key to not only relating but conveying the mission of the church as a body and as Christians individually. To understand the mission, we must understand that Jesus came incarnationally, in the flesh. That he came and dwelt among men. We too as a Christian Church, need to be incarnational in our communities where we live. We must become flesh to our neighbors and to the ones that we meet. The Christian Church is to share the lives, hopes and fears, pains, joys, culture, and language of the people to whom God has sent us to dwell with. The incarnational life means that church communities need to listen, understand, and fully enter the complex cultural reality of the area and people to which God has called us. Therefore, churches that serve in their area have a mission that looks different from other churches in another part of the country or another part of the state. It can even look different in different parts of the same town or city. Churches that realize that revitalization is needed within their congregation must also realize that it includes a plan and strategy that includes the community in which they are part of. There can be no true revitalization in a church that does not see the ones outside as an essential part of the future of the church.

A clearly stated mission must first start with an understanding that the work to be done is not a church-shaped mission, but a mission-shaped church. A mission-shaped church in any context recognizes that the mission is not an add-on activity, rather, it is the reason the church exists, the church is born through mission. This mission always comes from God the Father, through the Son and the power of the Holy Spirit. This pattern is the pattern of the ministry of Jesus in His incarnation.

Successful churches on a mission also understand the need to communicate the origin and value of their guiding mission. The stated mission is a clear expression of a church's reason for being that defines its primary long-term goal and direction. The mission statement often includes a plan of action for how to reach that goal. Mission is God finding those, whose hearts are right with Him and placing them where they can make a difference for His Kingdom. Some of the greatest missionaries ever recorded in history never lived long lives, but their lives drastically changed eternity for so many others. God had full access to Phillip, and the book of Acts gives the exciting account of how God used Phillips's life to take the gospel to the ends of the earth. Phillip was preaching powerfully in the city of Samaria (Acts 8:5). So powerfully and mighty did God use him that the entire city of Samaria was rejoicing at the miracles God was doing through Phillip (Acts 8:6-8). Any evangelist would give their right arm to have the same results that Phillip had, to see an entire city responding to the gospel through his preaching. Yet Phillip was not actively centered in his Christian life. He was God centered. He was on a mission for God. Phillip was not preoccupied with expanding his reputation as a great preacher or miracle worker. He was concerned that his life remains in the center of God's activity. When he was instructed to leave his fruitful ministry in the city, he did not hesitate (Acts 8:27).

God continues to seek those who are as responsive as Phillip was, to go on mission with Him. The reason God has not brought great revival to more places is not that He is unable or that He is unwilling. He first looks for those willing to have their lives radically adjusted away from their self-centered activities and placed into the center of God's activity around the world. Have you seen the activity of God around your church? What is God presently inviting your church to do? How is your church responding?[1]

Some of the strengths and accomplishments of the mission of Phillip were that he was one of the seven organizers of food distribution in the early church. He became one of the first traveling missionaries and evangelists for the gospel of Jesus Christ. He was one of the first to follow Jesus' command to take the gospel to all the people in all the land. And he was also a careful student of the Bible who could explain its meaning with clarity to all he met.

Phillip is a good example that God finds great and various uses for those willing to obey wholeheartedly to His call. Phillip shows the gospel is universal good news to everyone. The whole bible and not just the New Testament helps us understand more about who Jesus is. Phillip shows that both mass response, as in the Samaritans, and individual response, as in the Ethiopian man are valuable to God for the gospel of Jesus Christ.

Sanctify the Lord God in your heart, and always be ready to give a defense to everyone who asks you a reason for the hope that you have in you, with meekness and fear (1 Peter 3:15).

You may never know when it will happen. You might be on an airplane, at the office water cooler, in the backyard talking to a neighbor, in church, or in your children's room putting him or her to bed. There will be something, whether it'll be your kindness towards them, the other person's need, an event in the news, or a family problem, that may prompt the person to ask about your faith. Are you ready? What will you say? And how will you say it?

Questions about our faith may come in all kinds of varieties whether it be intellectual, ethical, or even personal, but at the bottom of it all, people want to know if our faith experience is rich and real and if it makes a difference in how we live. Man, did you get that! They are looking in you and, in your church, to see if they find anything different than they are seeing in the world and the stuff our culture has to offer. They are also looking for hope. They long to know they are loved, forgiven, and accepted by God, and they need someone to tell them that yes, it's true, God loves them too. Let us face the fact that the reason your church is needing revitalization is because somewhere along the way the church had forgotten that and stopped doing what they are called to do. We need to repent and turn to the One that is the reason we are who we are. Return to our first love (Rev. 2:4).

When the question is asked, it's too late to prepare our response and to prepare our hearts. We must get ready to answer the question by sanctifying Christ in our hearts, putting him first, above all other affections. When our love for Him transcends everything else in our lives, and even if we're actively struggling to love Him more than anything else, we are ready. Our words will reflect our heart, and authenticity is incredibly attractive to people. We don't argue people into the Kingdom, and we don't intimidate them into becoming God's beloved children. Peter reminds us that our demeanor should be with meekness and fear, realizing the awesome responsibility and privilege of communicating the light of the gospel to a darkened heart. This is mission. Are you ready? If someone asks you about your faith today, what would you say and how would you say it?

How would the church be different if we were known for telling people about Jesus and His love as well as showing people what Jesus did with that love? The world sees the church as a minority with an agenda. What the world should see is the love of God expressed through faithful missional living. We must be able to defeat the notions that many people have as Mark Twain once reportedly remarked, "church is good people standing in front of good people and telling them how to be good people." [2]

In the eyes of too many Christians, involvement in evangelism and missions is a good thing. But missional involvement for them it is not necessary to be a believer or even for the church to be the church. Nina Gunner, former director of Nazarene Missions International stated, "if you take missions out of the Bible, there is little left but the covers." The Great Commission is not an option to be considered, it is a command to be obeyed. Those who take scripture seriously understand that this Great Commission, also found in Mark 16:15, is the church's Kingdom calling.

> "Where there is no mission, there is no church, and where there is neither church nor mission, there is no faith... mission, gospel preaching, is the spreading out of the fire which Christ has thrown unto the earth. He who does not

propagate this fire shows that he is not burning. He who
burns propagates the fire."[3] – Emil Brunner, theologian

God is a missionary God, one who seeks and sends to find the lost.
After the fall, Adam and Eve hid in the garden, Scripture shows God
looking for them. God is seeking today. If God's people want to be part of
the mission, then they must see it as more than an option. We can read
passages like Romans 1:14-16 that puts mission at the very heart of what
the church is and does. If the church is to be truly the church, it must
operate, as Paul said to the Romans, *"by the command of the eternal God,
so that all nations might believe and obey Him"* (16:26).

Overcoming mission fatigue

For every reason that the Bible gives for congregations and individuals to
get involved and be missional there is the counter reaction of complacency
and missional fatigue. Missional fatigue can hinder efforts to mobilize
members from fulfilling The Great Commission. Visiting missionaries'
messages about God's heart and the needs of the world, no matter how
clearly illustrated and conveyed may not be enough to overcome the
deadening effects of mission fatigue. There are several factors that can
play into this paralyzing and debilitating fatigue.

1. **Inadequate understanding of church structure and purpose.** When
   the efforts of mission are seen as something outside the church or at
   best optional, then mission promotion becomes more of a fatigue and
   results in the listener tuning out and accepting less responsibility on
   their part. These people see themselves already committed enough
   to the cause around the world and that the church is doing enough
   already for missions, therefore turning a deaf ear to the cause. People
   like this are not going to be sensitive to the missional work until they
   stop seeing the church as a salad bar where you can pick and choose
   what and how much you want to do in the church's mission. That it
   is a matter of "take it or leave it" mentality.

2. **Lack of Facts.** People have a natural tendency to have a very low response to action if they do not have enough information to cause them to move. As a result of this inaction, people can seem to not care and may seem sinfully, or even apathetic, when the plain truth is that the people don't have enough information to cause them to want to act. People do not know what they are to pray for, so they do not pray at all for the cause, place, or people. They may not be aware there are missionaries that need prayer or support because the work is wearing them out or that they are being burnt out. They may not know large segments of the population are still unreached for the gospel of Christ. They may not be aware that the Holy Spirit is moving in mighty and powerful ways in a particular place. Maybe the information was not presented to them in a way they feel they can get involved in the ministry or for the missionary work. People need information to know that they can act. Many times, if they know what the need is and what the cause is for, people will respond in kind. So, the lack of action may be due to the lack of information provided to the listener. If we want people to respond to the call to missional, then we must be able to provide the appropriate and adequate information for people to be able to be part of that call.

3. **Selfishness.** Outright carnal selfishness plays the biggest part in missional fatigue. Today we live in a materialistic culture where everything is about what we can get. We find ourselves working long hours and working overtime at our jobs so that we can pay for our next toy or our next luxury that we can barely afford. Oftentimes, we can explain why we need a certain product or a particular luxury so that we can relax and enjoy ourselves. But when it comes to funding mission work or providing finance for a particular project, we find that we do not have the extra money to spare. We can't really afford to give anything right now for overseas mission work. We can't give money for the work of the homeless shelter down the street, or to help provide food for needy families in our community. It is easy to justify the things that we want but it is hard for many to part with the money to help others.

Outright selfishness has kept them from internalizing Jesus' words in Luke 14:33, *"those of you who do not give up everything you have cannot be my disciples."*[4]

For a church that is going through the revitalization process, that church must be a missional minded church. It is not something that is added onto the church, but it is the very DNA of the church. It is part of the identity of the church, being missional minded and having a missional heart. How would the church be different if we were known for telling people about Jesus and His love, as well as showing people what Jesus did with that love? The world sees the church as a minority with an agenda. What the world should see is the love of God expressed through faithful missional living throughout their church.

"Go therefore, and make disciples of all the nations, baptizing them in the name of the father and of the son and of the Holy Spirit." Matthew 28:19

Jesus commands us to go. We need permission to stay! The gospel accounts are accounts of Jesus leaving His Father's right hand to go to Calvary for us. Jesus told the ones that wanted to be His disciples that they had to leave their homes and their comforts to follow Him wherever He went. Some insisted that they could not go quite yet because they still had to take care of their elderly parent's back home (Luke 9:59-60). Others wanted to make sure everything was in order before they could leave (Luke 9:61-62). And then finally there were others that expressed willingness to follow Jesus but wanted to know the details of what they would be doing before they went (Luke 9:57-58). Jesus never excused those who struggled to follow Him. He made it clear that to follow Him meant they had to set their eyes and their minds upon Him and to let Jesus set the direction that they were to follow.

We can convince ourselves that Jesus doesn't really want us to adjust our lives, pointing to the success we are enjoying right where we are now. Yet Jesus often told His disciples to go elsewhere in spite of the success they were experiencing. Take for example Peter, who had just pulled in the greatest catch of fish of his entire career when Jesus invited him to leave everything to follow Him (Luke 5:1-11). Phillip was enjoying astonishing success as an evangelist in Samaria when the Holy Spirit instructed him to go to the desert to talk to an Ethiopian man (Acts 8:25-40). Success where we are can be our greatest hindrance to going where Jesus wants us to be, which is with Him and on mission for Him.

If you and your church become too comfortable where you are, you may resist Jesus' invitation to go where He is leading you. Don't assume God does not want you to go in service and on mission for Him. He may lead you across the street to share the gospel with your neighbor or He may send you to the other side of the world for people that do not know Him to hear the message of the cross. Wherever He leads, be prepared to go.

Telling Our Story

In the early years that I pastored our church, I was seeking God's guidance on how He wanted us to be on mission in our community. We were already serving a food ministry and working with the homeless in our neighborhood. But there was nagging in me that there was more. We were doing more than other churches, but I was reminded that we are not other places.

An opportunity came for a 3-day seminar for evangelism and discipleship in our district and I signed up for the studies. Going in I had the attitude that there was probably going to be some good information but did not expect anything ground shaking to result from it. The main reason I even went was because we were strongly urged by the Superintendent to attend. Most of it was what I pretty much expected, but one exercise stood out.

We were to come up with a plan, strategy, and target group for a church plant in our community. We had to work out the presentation and detail how we would launch this new church. While working on this project, it seemed that an idea emerged that God was prompting me to actually do this for our church. The idea was to have a children's church on the property of the apartment complexes in our community. In the culture that we live now, the time of inviting people to church and them coming has passed into history. So, instead of trying to get kids to come to our church, why don't we go to them where they live?

This is how NazKids came to be in existence. We go to two different apartment complexes of low-income housing, and we minister and conduct children's church for an hour and a half at each place. We have a traditional children's church with a meal at the end before they go home. Not only are we addressing their spiritual need but also addressing their physical need as well. In this way we are ministering to the whole person. This accomplished a couple of things at one time; we helped families with needs, and we were able to reach kids by going to them since the church did not have transportation to bring the kids to church. Everyone is benefits at the same time.

Reflection Questions

1. Can your church answer the question, what is your church trying to do? Who is your church trying to reach?
2. Does your church have a concise mission statement that defines your why and how?
3. How would your church be different if you were known for telling people about Jesus and His love as well as showing people what Jesus did with that love?

Best Practices/Ideas

1. Sit with your church leadership and write a precise mission statement for you church that answers your two questions of why and how.
2. If your church already has a mission statement, then revisit it and make sure it is still relevant now.
3. Make sure that the message of missions is an equal part of the church's whole message.

CHAPTER 8

Planning And Implementing the Strategy

And let us not grow weary while doing good, for in due season
we shall reap if we do not lose heart. Galatians 6:9

Guys, we must confess and own the fact we are known for trying to assemble and build things without using or reading the instructions that come with the product we just bought. It's a man's rite of passage to show the success of our effort without one time consulting the owner's manual even though there are leftover parts and screws left (I personally believe they pack extras just to throw us off).

We should be thanking God that the vision that He has placed in us through the prayerful guidance, and the mission that He has directed us in does not come without some kind of plan from Him. It is a popular saying that "God equips the ones that He calls." I totally believe this statement. I believe God will give you everything you need to fulfill the vision and mission that He places in you to complete the task fully.

God gave me the vision and the desired mission of NazKids in our community. The need was there, but the planning had to start before we could accomplish this task and go forward. The groundwork had to be done now. Things that needed to be addressed and marked off our to-do list included asking permission from the complex managers to hold NazKids on their property, who would be the workers and teachers, what curriculum were we to use, what equipment did we need, and plenty of other little details. Plans of how things were to work is critical for success in ministries, especially in the beginning stages.

We spent many Wednesday and Sunday evenings talking and planning the logistics. Some thought that we over thought it, but when you plan well everything works and flows much better. After all the preparation the time had come to launch NazKids. We went to the properties and set up, we held children's church right where they live. The turnout was great. A couple weeks prior to the launch we made flyers that we placed on doors and at the mailboxes for everyone to see. We also had yard signs made up that we placed in the spot that we were planning to use to tell them NazKids was coming. On the day of the event, we knocked on doors and told them that NazKids was here!

The first NazKids had 35+ kids and parents come to participate. Throughout the year we ended up having an average of 30-50 people come and be a part of NazKids. Because of the nature of the service we conducted there, we were able to register the two complexes as PAC's with our denomination which counted toward attendance and outreach. PAC's are "Parent Affiliated Congregations" which count as church plants. So not only did we reach new families that we had not before but now we had two new church congregations. This made us a multiplying church. The Kingdom is being expanded and we are the workers and servants for the King.

Servants of Jesus Christ the King.

The servant carries out the master's will. The servant doesn't tell the master what to do. The servant does not choose which task to perform for the master, nor does the servant suggest days or times when it would be convenient to serve the master. The servant's function is to follow instructions. The master, on the other hand, gives directions. The master does not tell the servant to develop a vision that will guide the master. The master is the one with the vision, the servant's task is to help fulfill the master's purpose.

We are the servants; God is the master. We tend to try to reverse this. God's revelation of Himself, His purposes, and His ways depends directly upon our obedience. He may not reveal today His intentions for the next five years, but He will tell us what our next step should be. As we respond to God's revelation, He will accomplish what He desires, He will be the one who receives the glory.

Our fulfillment comes from serving our Master.

The world will encourage you to strive for positions of authority and power. God wants you to take the role of a servant. As God's servants you should have no other agenda than to be obedient to whatever He tells you. God does not need you to dream great dreams for your life, your family, your business, or your church. He simply asked for obedience. He has plans that would dwarf yours in comparison (Eph. 3:20).

When it comes to revitalization of a church very few have a strategy in how to implement the vision and mission given to them. As a result, most flip and flop around with no direction or plan like a fish out of the water. Most churches trying to revitalize and trying to get the fire started in the church again, shoot blindly into the dark hoping to hit something that will work or make them feel better about themselves. Although every church and every community are different, I believe there are some solid suggestions that can be given for every revitalization effort.

Realizing that the church is unhealthy

I know that this seems like a no-brainer but there are too many churches that want to be and do the healthy church things without acknowledging that they are sick and need a physician desperately. Revitalization is steering a church from the unhealthy choices and lack of discipline to a church that is chasing after Jesus and leading lost people to the Kingdom, this is what matters. Nothing that your church does matters, as far as Sunday School, children's programs, outreach, or even overseas missions if it does not work toward bringing people into the Kingdom. Unhealthy churches are me-centered and not Kingdom-centered. To take a church that is sick and to turn it to a healthy church takes purposeful work with a goal in view. A reason for being and doing.

Be intentional. And then, be intentional some more.

Success, in all areas of life, usually comes as the result of careful planning and hard work. When it comes to breathing new fire within the church, many are simply carried along by whatever wave happens to pick them up. This leads to churches with little success and smaller amounts of engagement.

Although the church leadership may choose to support half a dozen random ideas of ministry, in half a dozen locations, doing half a dozen different kinds of ministry, does the congregation even know the programs or workers exist? Does anyone have a connection to their ministry? Are the workers thriving in the ministry they were sent to accomplish? We must be intentional about every aspect, of every area that we need to move in. There must be careful thought followed by even more intentional action. Tony Morgan in his book "The Unstuck Church" says, "Plan your work and work your plan." [3]

All too often, a church's revitalization strategy develops in isolation, away from the mission and vision of the church. More with the pastor or at best with the board, while everyone else is left out of the discussion. It is rarely run through the lens of the church's vision and focus. In this you end up with pockets of ministry instead of intentional thought-out planning.

Instead, wouldn't it be better if we approached any revitalization effort in the same way we approach starting a youth group, worship team or local church plant? With intentionality, creativity, critical thought, and careful planning? If we approach the church revitalization strategy the same way, would we be more effective? We would certainly stand a better chance of success and fulfilling what the Lord had revealed to us in the first place?

The renewed fire should be an outgrowth of local missions.

There is sometimes an unwritten assumption in churches that the development of a revitalization strategy should be left to the "experts," and, so goes the thinking, the local church isn't an "expert." I feel compelled to fight this series of beliefs. Local churches should inherently be the expert in their particular city or neighborhood. The fire starts at home. Churches going through the revitalization process should be looking at what God is already doing in your town or local.

So, why not ask the people that are already around you and that you may be already serving in some way, to identify their needs and hopes. Instead of assuming what they need, let them tell you. We must have compassion for the ones that we want to serve but that compassion must give birth to strategy. Through this you are more likely to see fruit being produced from the seeds you plant and water.

Let me give you some practical examples. I pastor a church that has two very visible areas of focus when it comes to local ministry: We minister to individuals that suffer from food insecurity, and we minister to the homeless in our neighborhood. On both the local and global fronts, we support individuals and other organizations who are working with people that need food, and we support individuals who work with the outcast, the underprivileged and the destitute. When we looked around and did not take very long before we could see the need that was all around us. In seeing that need we were able to step inand help people of all ages. We still ask questions about what their needs may be because that is a fluid situation for many. If a person has a need in one area, say food insecurity, then there will be others needs that they will have. Things like trouble affording their meds because of lack of money or fixed income. Many times, the needs can change according to the seasons. People have more needs in the winter staying warm versus the summer. People have less need at tax return time rather than the holidays. We must be ready to adjust the strategy as need changes.

Boundaries or city limits matter very little.

Sometimes we are very quick to say that person or that group of people live in this place or closer to that church, so we will not go there. The truth is that all people everywhere are our responsibility. If God has placed someone in your path or God has opened a door for you and your church to minister, then you need to walk through that opportunity. It could very well be that you and your church have special gifts or resources to help these people and that is the reason that God directed them to you. Don't put boundaries on the work of your church. The revitalization has much more to do with the act of engaging the un-gospeled people, wherever we find them, with the good news of Christ's kingdom. I encourage churches to build their strategies around mission type first and ministry location second.

Building relationships.

If you don't have a revitalization strategy, you're very much in danger of paralysis by analysis, as there are too many good options to know where to begin. Without a plan in place with first steps then second and so on then the process can get stuck in planning, talking it to death in committee meetings, and more discussions without ever really doing anything. Some can get the feeling that they are really making progress because they have talked about it so much and had meetings on the planning, that they start thinking they are really gaining traction and moving forward, when in reality they have never left their seats.

If you are questioning where to start the process, look around and see if there is any connection to the church community that you are already in. This is the best place to start, where you're already making and connecting in relationships. Building and nurturing those contact points is the place to start.

Start with relationships in the church itself. There are relationships within the church walls that can be improved or built upon that can help. Relationships that need mending in your congregation. There is hardly a church out there that can not benefit from this relationship mending and building.

Building relationships with people outside the church that you already know and build upon those. You may have a good acquaintance with the shop owner down the street that you know does not go to church anywhere, you can build an even better relationship with them where you can have conversations that are Kingdom centric. Maybe the mechanic that does your oil changes can be someone that you can build on past the talks about the needs of your car. There are opportunities all around us if we just look at the fields.

When laying out and praying about the strategy and plan that your church is going to take in fulfilling what God has revealed to you and your church, be very deliberate and intentional about everything. Don't think that you must do everything. Be prepared to go into the areas that God has laid on your hearts to minister in.

Consider leading your congregation through an intentional season of prayer for the community around the church. As you do so, ask yourself these questions:

Who does the Lord keep bringing to our minds?

Do we gravitate toward any particular places or kinds of ministries?

Who do we already know who is working in those kinds of ministries or places?

What are the greatest needs that are within our fingertips?

Where do we see God already moving?

What is Holding You Back?

In every revitalization effort there is the sense of moving forward, making plans for what to do, and how we take the next steps. But you also must look at the things that may hold you back and cause you resistance. You need to look at what limiting factors that may be holding you back from completing the vision God has called you to do. Give your leadership team the permission to speak openly and honestly about any obstacles that they may see from you completing the mission. If someone mentions a factor that may hinder the mission plan, let them also explain why it is a limitation. If the suggestion is valid, then write it or record it so that the leadership can look at it and address it to solve or work around it. There are unlimited reasons why one thing or another may not work, or at least bring difficulty in carrying out, but there are some universal reasons why strategies do not come to fruition in many churches. Some would be:

- No consensus or passion for the direction the church is going. If leadership has not clearly and effectively conveyed the vision, mission, strategy, and success measurement then it is hard for people to get onboard. Church members want their leaders to clearly articulate why they exist as a church (mission). They want clarity on what foundational convictions will guide the ministry (values). Then they want to understand the intentional process that will be employed to involve all the members and meaningful ministry (strategy).[1]
- No plan and process for making disciples. Many churches think about reaching out, and bringing people in, but the work of discipling and raising up people to make disciples falls short. In some cases, the process is not even thought about. What good does it do to lay out a strategy to revitalize a church and reach new people if we do not walk them through their walk with the Lord and grow in grace with them.
- Another good sign that your strategy plan needs adjusting is when guests don't come back after visiting. This is a serious matter that holds any church back from revitalization. Most people will decide if they will return to the church within the first few minutes of the first visit. Factors that may hold you back are there enough people to greet and welcome people in, signage and information to help direct the guest, and cleanliness and appearance of the church. All these and most can hold back the plan of the church.

- Is there enough and adequate connection points, as in small groups, for people to make that connection? Prayer groups and house meetings are other great ways to fight off the things that hold back churches from implementing their strategy for ministry in effective ways. Have ways that people can connect and build relationships. Without relationships being built then the plans, strategies, and the church cease to be effective for anybody.

What Strategic Planning Should Clarify and Do for a Church

I know that the concept of "Church/Ministry Strategy" can sound a bit corporate-esque but that is the essential component of moving a church from plateau and decline to sustainable health and growth. The question is often asked, why should you work on your ministry strategy and build action plans? There's a very good biblical reason for it: When you make vision actionable, you can empower people in your congregation to do the work of the ministry.

When communicating the vision, make it plain for everyone to understand and be able to replicate easily: Where are we going and how are we going to get there? The win here, for this phase of the process is that you define a 5-Year Vision with measurable goals and a clear path forward for action. The focus is on getting you executing and achieving wins in the first 90 days.

1. **You go back to foundational biblical truths to clarify your purpose as a church. Answering who we are.**
   Starting with Scripture and a focused time of prayer, you will reflect on your purpose and the biblical reason and call for why you exist as a church.
2. **Explore your ministry's reach—today and its potential—based on where God has placed your church.**
   Utilizing all available reports and data on the demographics of your specific community, you can clarify exactly who is in your mission field within the full reach of your church. Through

discussions with your own church's leadership, talking with other churches, government leaders, school resource councilors, you'll be able to identify who you believe God has called you to reach, what's important to them, and how your church will respond.

3. **Build your Discipleship Path.**

Find a common language to answer the question *"What is a disciple?"* as well as a shared understanding of how your church will help people take their next steps towards Christ. This is a crucial part of the strategy plan because it is one thing to get them in but helping them grow is the future life of the church.

4. **Recognize your Growth Engines and place the right champions for each effort.**

Determine the 3-4 core growth engines of your church— the ministries, events and/or strategies that help you grow your Kingdom impact and reach more people. You will need to identify a champion for each growth engine and map out a plan for next steps to grow your reach within them.

5. **Craft a 5-Year Vision.**

Your leadership will shape a clear and specific vision for where you believe God is calling the church to be five years from now.

6. **Identify 3-5 key behaviors you need reflected in your church to drive the culture you are trying to create within the congregation.**

The leadership of the church must talk and live out the expected culture that you are trying to create within the people of the church. You are wanting the vision to be part of the DNA of the body of Christ in your local context.

7. **Build a system to monitor church health.**

Creating a way and standard for measuring the progress and success of the strategy.

8. **Break down everything that needs action to accomplish the future vision.**

Prioritize the three action steps you need to take over the next three months. In this part of the process, develop a regular 90-Day Action Plan cycle of follow-through, so that you begin creating greater accountability for action. This helps you teach your people how to execute on quarterly cycles. Keeping the momentum going in the right direction and in a timely manner.

9. **Finding a coach or a mentor that has been through the process can help as you lead change.**

   Your plans will likely involve the need to lead your congregation through some significant changes throughout the process. Coaching for your leaders and sharing best practices as you begin implementing your plan will greatly improve the likelihood of success.

Telling our Story

In my church, I saw very early on that God was showing me that the congregation needed to understand more clearly who they were and what they were in Jesus Christ. I wholeheartedly believe that we do not understand who we are as a people of God when we cannot have a clear understanding of what our purpose is in the Kingdom of God.

> *"Blessed is the man who trusts in the Lord, and whose hope is the Lord. For he shall be like a tree planted by the waters, which spreads out its roots by the river, and will not [a]fear when heat comes; But its leaf will be green, and will not be anxious in the year of drought, Nor will cease from yielding fruit" (Jeremiah 17:7-8).*

I saw that our need was depth, not just how many we had in the church. Revitalization can actually spark fire within the church when they understand more clearly who and Who's they are. When identity is lost or distorted then purpose is lost or distorted as well. The uncertainty of who we are causes called purpose to drift from the center, and left unchecked and uncorrected it will lead to areas never intended to be dwelled in. No church happens accidentally. There is intention and purpose driving the new congregation of believers. But time seems to cause us to drift and slackness creeps in slowly and undetected. We all become complacent in our worship, satisfied with tradition and status quo. The fire in the belly grows cold without the coals being stoked like a blacksmith's furnace. The church finds itself saying, "we had no idea where we were going or what we were doing."

For far too long the small church has bought a bill of goods that does not need to be true. They have bought into the assumption that since they are small then they must be insignificant. When we understand who we are as a church we are more able to see and respond to the needs of our community.

The church I shepherd, no longer had a sense of direction or purpose other than existing for another month. It was not until we sat down and started to understand again who we were and for what purpose that we existed for that we started moving forward again. Some will be content to just show up on Sundays and sing their 6 songs that they always sing and hear a message that does not challenge or stretch me. But for the church to have a fire that God intends then there must be a Holy Ghost movement within our souls to be everything God wants for that church that you attend.

Reflection Questions

1. Does your church have a plan for carrying out the vision and mission that God has placed in you?
2. Has the strategy of your church been successful in accomplishing the mission? If so, how? If not, why?
3. What are the next steps to take to advance the Kingdom even further in your neighborhood?

Best Practices/Ideas

1. Sit with the church leadership and examine your ministry strategy and see if there is any area that needs revised or overhauled.
2. Formulate a strategy that is Kingdom-centric and is not church-centric.
3. Ask questions of people that you may be serving already, along with other community agencies to see what they say is the greatest need. Adjust your planning around those responses.

Putting Our Money Where Our Mouth Is

*"His lord said unto him, Well done, thou good and faithful
servant: thou hast been faithful over a few things, I will make thee
ruler over many things: enter thou into the joy of thy lord."*
(Matt. 25:14)

*"Do not withhold good from those to whom it is
due, when it is in your power to act."*
(Proverbs 3:27)

Investment into the mission is possibly one of the most difficult paths to navigate but is, without doubt, the most important. Amazingly, people will feel comfortable enough to tell you all sorts of things about them from the slightest ill-thought they may have had about someone, to moral failures that break up homes and marriages, but when it comes to money or finances, they will quickly tell you it is none of your business. It is as if the topic of money and finances somehow became an unspoken rule that we do not talk about. In our experience, people are more comfortable talking about their sex lives than they are about their finances. One of the main reasons for this, is because people have not been taught how to handle money God's way.

The world tells us that we should live beyond our means, use other people's money (credit), and save as little as possible because it doesn't really matter. God's Word tells us the opposite. We are to be good stewards of what He has entrusted to us. That includes our time, our talents, and our finances. When it comes to financial giving, people will give all sorts of excuses why they cannot or why they do not want to. We have heard every excuse in the book. The truth is, if we are honest with ourselves, we can usually find a way to make it happen if we really want to.

Another scenario is talking about vision, mission, and strategy. implementation is fine until we mention what it will cost to do the things to move the church forward. Many times, the treasurer will chinch the purse strings as if it was their pocket that you are reaching into. Once you have established a plan and strategy for implementing the vision and mission of the church the next step is to establish a financial plan. Your hopes and prayers won't pay the bills. In scripture it says, but don't begin until you count the cost. Who would begin construction of a building without first calculating the cost to see if there is enough money to finish it? Otherwise, you might complete only the foundation before running out of money, and then everyone would laugh at you. They would say, there's the person who started that building and couldn't afford to finish it! (Luke 14:28-30)

In the discipline of stewardship, planning is an essential element. If we don't plan, we run the risk of wasting resources on initiatives that might not be God's priority for the church. Regardless of the strategy that you and your leadership developed, regardless of how extensive or how thorough it may be, you will not accomplish the mission if it does not have the funding to back it. The common response to this is, that God will provide. And He will, but part of His provision is you and me being good stewards and handling our finances in a way that honors Him. It starts with each of us as individuals deciding to be obedient to what He has called us to do. If we want to see the mission of the church accomplished, we must be willing to put our money where our mouth is.

There are at least three areas of finances that need to be considered for funding. There needs to be a bucket for the initial startup cost, the ongoing cost supported by giving, and support for the initial gap from outside sources.

1. **Initial startup cost.** The first area is for all the money needed to cover one-time startup costs. It's going to be different for every church, but that might include remodeling, new or updated audio and video equipment, children's ministry equipment, facility renovations, and so on. You need to have funding in place before you start the new project to cover these expenses. You may need to invest in additional staff to cover an area of ministry that you are leading into. Perhaps you need to invest money into that church van that needs repairs and new tires and maybe invest in a new van period. These costs can be anything that it will take to get the ministry rolling and the revitalization effort underway so that the church can proceed. If nothing is spent and nothing is invested things will most likely stay the way, they have always been.

2. **Ongoing cost supported by faithful giving.** This next area to consider is the money that comes in through faithful giving of the ones that have bought into the vision and mission of the church. For this money, you need to have plans for that money of where it is going to be spent. The reason that you must have a plan is that there is not going to be very much money in the early days coming in. When people are new to the church or are coming from a different faith their giving will be less than that of a long-time member. It is an obvious conclusion that you will have to do some ministering to those people, but don't expect them to financially contribute right away.

   For these reasons, you need to have a plan and a budget in place for how you're going to spend this limited number of finances that will be available to you. Be sure to plan before you launch this new effort, and you may need to make modifications based on the actual giving experience week to week. A good word of advice would be to plan to spend less in this area. It is hoped that this buffer zone of giving, and spending will help relieve some of the stress in the long run and free up dollars to follow God's leading.

3. **Filling the gap by outside sources.** This source of giving comes in through your church's giving and is what is legitimately required to sustain the ministry through the revitalization process. It would

be very unlikely that a church would be self-sustaining from day one. It may take several years for a church to be able to support all the finances needed for the revitalization effort. Part of your fundraising before and after the church starts this effort, must be coming from a third area and source.

If you have been diligent to plan, you've already recognized that two of the three areas don't involve people at your church. That may mean you have to consider several other options:

- You may need to find a second job and be bi-vocational for a season. This is not the ideal situation to be in, but many do that during the initial phases of a church revitalizing and needing extra funds. You may need to find an evening or weekend job to help supplement the mission. And there likely will be times that you will need to step out in faith and give up that extra paycheck when the revitalization effort requires more full-time attention from your leadership.
- You may need to save more money before you start. This assumes you're out of debt. Debt without question limits our ability to say yes to the calling Jesus has for our lives and for steps into revitalization that requires funding. You may have to take steps that require little to no money to initiate. Prayer is the first thing that needs to happen so that is the first step for the revitalization effort.
- You may need to have your ministry leaders raise their support. There are plenty of ministries all over the world that use this strategy to fund their mission. It means sacrificing time and energy to raise support, but don't make it a long-term solution.
- You may need to ask other churches, your denomination, or your district superintendent for support. Many districts and church advisory boards have money and grants that can be invested into not only church plants, but also in helping churches to revitalize. This requires you to be able to sit down with other leaders and disseminate the vision, the mission and what God is calling your church to do to make a case for support.

To go a little deeper into the subject of raising support by faithful giving of your people, you will need to talk to them, and teach them what the Bible says about faithful giving. I'd begin by letting people know that God and His church don't want their money. God wants their hearts. What is interesting, is that Jesus said, "wherever your treasure is, there the desires of your heart will be also" (Matthew 6:21).

If I were Jesus, I would have reversed that statement completely around. I would have said, "wherever the desire of your heart is, there your treasure will be also." In other words, when God has your heart, He'll also be in control of how you use your money. The way that Jesus taught it is just the complete opposite. When we fully trust God with our money, our heart for God follows. People need to hear that over and over and over.

Every Church that is going through the revitalization effort and wants to move into the next phase of the life cycle must have a plan to fund the mission. For the church to become self-sustaining, you must begin establishing this foundation from the very beginning.

Different people are in different stages with their financial stability. Here are some thoughts to consider when talking to people about finances:

- Some people have money problems. If you don't state the obvious, they're going to assume you've completely disconnected from their reality and their financial situation. If this is a challenge people are facing in their private lives, why not teach them what the Bible says on this issue?
- Encourage everyone to participate. From the very start of the revitalization effort, the need is for everyone to participate in the giving. Regardless of how small or how big, the widow's offering of two small coins is just as important to the health of the church as it is to the larger amounts that others may be able to give. It is a matter of faithfulness and generosity. Everyone needs to be encouraged to participate.
- Give people a chance to share their stories. There are going to be times when people will need to express and testify to the fact of how their hearts have changed when they began to give God control of their finances. These testimonies are valuable to the

church not only spiritually but for encouraging giving and faithful giving by other people.

- Encourage people to volunteer. Serving creates ownership and the mission. Research shows that people who volunteer also give more to the mission than anyone else. When they are bought in, they will give to the cause of the revitalization effort. It cannot be overstated buy-in is essential for moving the needle forward.
- Be intentional with your offering times. Take a few minutes during each service to teach giving, a truth found in scripture, a story of life change, or a connection to the church's mission and vision. People need to know they are part of a cause much bigger than themselves.

Hope will not pay the bills even though we should have hope it cannot be placed in finances, it must be placed in God. Prayer will not pay your salary although you should certainly pray for God's provision for your salary. You need to be doing what the Bible says that you should be doing. You need to count the cost, and you need to plan before you build.

Bill Henard wrote in an article about the importance of buy-in in your congregation. He suggested you must have buy-in for the process to move forward. Buy-in is the beginning point of revitalization and it is the ending point as well. The reason is that it does not matter how well a church's leadership plans and strategies for revitalization, if the church is not on board and ready to learn to embrace the changes necessary to give them and keep them on a growth plane, all the work will be in vain. This coming on board and embracing the changes requires funding from the church and its members. We spend our money on what our hearts love the most. If we are truly committed to the revitalization of our church and our community then we must be willing to open our wallets, checkbooks, and debit cards to the cause of reaching lost people.

Some will ask where is the return on my investment? Your return is knowing that the work of the Kingdom is being done and in such a way that souls are being brought into the Kingdom. How is buy-in and investment in the Kingdom achieved? The following steps will help us to navigate the treacherous waters of finances.

- Talk with people. Dealing with emotions and people's pocketbooks can be a tricky area to try and navigate. Share details with people involved in the investment that you want them to make. Caring for them as if they're part of your immediate family. Avoid speaking to them with speeches and have a real dialogue with them. Think through the following guidelines for healthy conversations:

  * Quantity – give enough information but do not inundate people. Leave them feeling informed.
  * Quality - be completely genuine and honest and do not embellish the information.
  * Relational - be relevant and communicate how the change will affect people personally and what will be expected of them.
  * Manner - be clear, brief, and logical; avoid being vague, ambiguous, and wordy.

People are more likely to invest in the ministry and the efforts of the church if they feel that they are fully informed and have a significant role to play in the outcomes.

- Address the emotions in the room. Work to understand how church members and leaders are feeling about the investment that they are being asked to put their money into. Emotions and hesitation are often triggered by lack of information, new expectations, a lack of structure or certainty, feeling threatened, and being comfortable with the status quo, and not wanting to change. Create acceptance, commitment, hope, and trust by letting people deal with their hesitations and questions, not just facts. For example, people know that the church is declining. Those are the facts. The emotion, however, is a sense of guilt or a fear of the unknown and the future. They need to be able to work through these uncertainties and with your help, guidance and patience so they can become a great asset for the investment in the Kingdom. Sometimes it just takes time.

- Communicate, repeat, communicate, repeat. The leaders who create the need for change fail to understand the frequency of communication that is necessary for people to understand it emotionally, intellectually, and in this case financially. As people deal with their emotions, they are less receptive to believing what they hear. Consistency and repetition are key to helping people fight the anxiety that goes along with finances.[1]

- Vary the medium of communication. When people hear the same message from multiple directions, it has a better chance of being heard and remembered, on both intellectual and emotional levels. So, as we stand in pulpits, we need to reiterate the importance of funding the mission. In our newsletters and bulletins, we need to print the work and the funds needed to accomplish that work. In our board meetings and our informal conversations, one on one, we need to be talking about the mission and what is needed to help carry that mission forward.

"Whenever" We Give

"Take heed that you do not do your charitable deeds before men, to be seen by them. Otherwise, you have no reward from your Father in heaven. Therefore, when you do a charitable deed, do not sound a trumpet before you as the hypocrites do in the synagogues and in the streets, that they may have glory from men. Assuredly, I say to you, they have their reward. But when you do a charitable deed, do not let your left hand know what your right hand is doing, that your charitable deed may be in secret; and your Father who sees in secret will Himself reward you openly. (Matt. 6:1-4).

I think there is some good advice that we can receive from these verses, and there is a whole lot that can be said because of these verses. We could talk about how Jesus is aware of our abilities to twist the right actions that we are intended to carry out into wrong motives that we serve towards self-satisfaction. We could talk about our leaning toward the fact that we want to be liked and well thought of by those around us. We could talk about the potential insincerity lurking in all our hearts as the praise of God competes with the praise of men for how much we give and how we give it. But before coming to all that let's take and pay attention to one word in verse 2.

Whenever.

Not "if" or "in case," but "whenever." This is the word that Jesus uses when addressing our generosity and willingness to give materially to help those that are in need and to fund the mission of the church.

Whenever.

This is an important note to take because it shows that when Jesus is telling us to "whenever we give," he is assuming that Christ-followers will be givers. That we will be generous. So, he doesn't bother to tell us to give, he assumes we already are, and wants to instruct us on the nature of that giving. Generosity, for the Christian, ought to be ingrained into the fabric of who we are and embedded into our DNA. It should simply be a part of our regular operation daily in our life without Having to think about it.

There are times in our walk that we struggle with generosity and with giving. We wonder things like:

- Will we have enough if we are to give this portion of money away for mission work?
- Will we be satisfied if we are forced to live on what is left after we give?
- Will the amount that we are giving even make a difference in the mission?

These are some good questions. These are valid questions. They're not questions that excuse us from the generosity of giving, but they are questions that can and should be answered. The answers are found in the character of God. Specifically, certain attributes of God fuel our generosity. Let us look at three:

1. **God is faithful.** God's faithfulness is the fuel for our generosity. When Jesus told us to pray, he told us to pray for our daily bread. Not tomorrow's bread; not retirement bread; but daily bread. When we give in this way, we can do it with a supreme degree of confidence because of God's faithfulness himself. We can pray with joy knowing that God will give us what we need, when we need it.

   We can look behind us throughout our lives and see a whole host of examples of God's faithfulness in our past. We can see examples of His faithfulness when we were aware of Him and when we were not. When we prayed, and even when we didn't. We also remember when He gave us what we asked for and when He delivered something we didn't think we wanted at the time. But in all these cases, He has been faithful.

   The question of will we have enough is not answered by our wise planning or clever strategies, but it's answered by faith in God's continuing faithfulness.

2. **God is generous.**

   We may, as we are contemplating our commitment to being generous, question whether we will be able to be satisfied with less. We wonder if we are giving too much and will we fall short and other needs of life. We will have less money to live on if we give some away, so can we be satisfied with what is left? The answer is yes, and it's yes because of the generosity of God.

   One of the greatest lies that we tend to believe over and over again from the enemy is that God is holding out on us and is trying to deprive us of something better. It is, in fact, the same lie that the serpent fed to Eve on the day of the fall. The same lie that he told her that there is another tree that has the best fruit, and this best fruit is what God is keeping from you and depriving you of. So, it is with us. We look at our jobs, our families, and our incomes, and we build up a belief that God is holding out on us. And yet the truth is completely the opposite.

God is not holding out on us because there is nothing left for Him to hold out. He has already given us every spiritual blessing in Christ (Ephesians 1:3). The fact that God the Father bankrupts heaven to give us His very best, Jesus Christ our Lord, should tell us that the Father has given us the very best gift from heaven. The generosity of God in Christ fuels our generosity because we are reminded that no matter how much we give away, we are rich in Jesus Christ.

3. **God is intentional.** God is Many things, but he is not arbitrary. He is intentional. He does things on purpose and for a reason. What we have, we have because God has seen fair to give it to us, intentionally. Take, for example, Jesus' parable of the talents. One of the things you noticed straight away in the story is that the landowner gives different amounts to the servants (Matthew 25:14). The same is true for God.

   Let me encourage you, you have what you have because God intentionally decided you ought to have what you have. The intentionality of God fuels our generosity because it reminds us that we have been entrusted with specific things, and specific amounts, for the sake of the Kingdom. If God is this purposeful, then we also must be intentionally generous.

   So how much should you give to the revitalization effort of your church and its mission, and the missions that are involved in that process? I don't know. But whatever that amount is, don't let it be a grudgingly random amount. Instead, allow the truth of who God is to fuel your passion for generosity for the work of revitalization. We need to be putting money where our mouth is. If we know that our church needs revitalization and we do not contribute funds and resources towards that effort, then we are just as responsible if the church closes and dies, because we sat back and did nothing because of a few coins. Let God greatly bless you today by blessing the effort of the church.[2]

Telling our Story

As it was stated in earlier chapters the church that has become my home was flat busted and broke when I became pastor. The only thing that saved the church from financially sinking to the bottom, was selling a piece of property to a member that was interested in the small lot and house that was on it. It was not a huge sum of money, but it did pay off a loan from the bank that they had only been making interest payments on for quite some time. After that loan was cleared, we next caught up on all budgets and allocations that had fallen behind for several years. We needed to make good on all the things that we were obligated to do from the beginning. It is my belief and conviction that God will not honor and bless us the way that we needed if we were behind in our debts. For That matter, it is an integrity issue. If we are slack on some things, then how can we expect to be respected by others?

After all the debts were paid and everything was caught up and current, the next step that we took was to look at how we were going to invest in ministry and outreach. We took a deliberate look at ways that we could invest in the community and neighbors. We set aside money for two block parties for the first year. Through those block parties, we were able to get over 450 people to come and participate in the festivities. We had registration tables as they came in so that we could draw names for prizes, giveaways, and most importantly names and contact info so that we could follow up and invite people to church. There was not a great influx of people coming to the church, but what it did do was let the community know that we were still alive and kicking.

We intentionally set aside and spent money in areas that got us out of the church doors and into the neighborhood and community at large. We invested in helping schools that needed help with less fortunate students. We bought and provided school supplies, bought food for after-school backpacks filled with food, and special projects for special needs students. It is the same concept as investing in the stock market or your 401k. You put money in again and again and again for quite a while before you see much return on your investment. Look at investing in schools like investing in the stock market or any other investment opportunity. The return will come, and God will honor that investment, days, weeks, or maybe even years down the road.

Because of our investment and not hoarding the money that comes in, God has blessed us in such a tremendous way. In 2016 and 2017 the church brought in through tithes and offerings a whopping $35,000 each year. In 2022 the church doubled the giving to $70,000. It is not because the church has greatly grown in attendance, but I believe because of our faithfulness and commitment to fulfilling our obligations. The amazing thing is that during the time the church being closed to in-person meetings for 2 months, and with the pandemic all through 2020, the church received tithes, offerings and grants for the ministry that we were already doing, over $100,000, and we raised 12,000 for a bus to expand our children's ministry in the same year. I don't know about you but that is God stuff there.

The point in all this is, that God will honor and bless you, your church, and your ministry if we are willing to fund the church in areas that need backing with finances. Don't hang on to too much money in the church bank account. Budget money, enough money for the work God is calling you into in your community. Invest in your neighbors and in your community. The return will be more than any human can imagine or think of. The investment will be eternal.

Reflection Questions

1. Does your church have money that sits in the bank account not being used? If so, why?
2. Be willing to invest in the community? What areas need your attention for giving?
3. Is your church teaching giving regularly?

Best Practices/Ideas

1. Invest in the school system, health services, other non-profits, and any underserved need.
2. Fund-raisers can create excitement for the mission and funds to feed the mission work.
3. Teach your church about the story of the talents.

CHAPTER 10

Witnessing Is a Privilege and Responsibility

*"That which we have seen and heard we declare to you, that you
also may have fellowship with us; and truly our fellowship is
with the Father and with His Son Jesus Christ." (1 John 1:3)*

The word witness is interesting since it denotes something that we are and something we do. One who sees or experiences something is a witness, and one who tells about that is witnessing. It is clear that all who see or experience something are witnesses, and it is also clear that not all witnesses are witnessing. If you are a Christian, you are a witness. How good and faithful of a witness are you?

We need to be identified by love and the fact that we have a mission that shows through our actions and a witness that we can tell others. As Christians with a message of hope to give everyone in the world, we need to be demonstrating the joy that is in our hearts. It should be showing up on our faces and in our attitudes. But unfortunately, many times we run across Christians, born-again believers, that are anything but joyful and show anything but love. I don't know why so many unhappy people that we meet are our church people? If we think about it some believers seem to think that being unhappy and complaining is the mark of being a mature older Christian. But that should not be the case, nor should it be the defining mark of a Christian or a church. Instead, it should be the connection of love to everyday life that should identify the church and the

Christian as ones that Christ has sent to make a difference in this world. There lies our witness and our testimony.

It is not hard to find data and surveys that reinforce the argument that a large number of people do not go to church anymore because the members of the church where they attended seemed to be judgmental or hypocritical. Many didn't feel as if they were connected to the people in the church. And there are even numbers that suggest that people quit coming to church because people were either unfriendly, unwelcoming, or cliquish. Many times, we describe someone or identify someone by a characteristic that is prominent in that person. If we are talking about a particular person that we know is prone to be short and blunt, then we call them grumpy. You know Mr. Bill down the street is a grumpy old man, or we might say Mrs. Jones next door is a sweet old lady. People are described by their attitudes and characteristics.

That is why it is curious that God is known and described as love, but Christians who are the children and heirs to the throne can be anything but love to people that see them and witness their life. In their book "Compelled by Love" by Ed Stetzer and Philip Nation, they say about God,

"Scripture isn't saying He is a loving God although He is. It isn't saying that when we think about love, we need to think about God. Neither is it saying God is like love. Rather, God is love. Therefore, the love born from His being is not earthly by nature; it isn't human or common: it is divine love."[1]

The church is to be known as an extension of God's character; it is to be known as love. As Christians when our day is done and our family and friends gather around us, I would hope, those who knew us would say that we look like God, who is love. We should be like the child that goes to school and takes something with them at the show and tell. We should be living our lives as if we are taking Jesus with us everywhere and that we are willing to tell everyone about Jesus through our words and our lives. We should be excited just like the child that stands up before the class to show off what they have brought for show and tell. We also should be standing before a world that does not know Christ, that is lost and undone and standing in the darkness, telling them about the light and love of Christ that can be in their life. So, our lives ought to be a show and tell life before others. How wonderful would it be if the church were known for telling people about Jesus and His love as well as showing people what Jesus did with His love in our lives?

We know that love is the very heart of God. In response to this love, what is the church to do? The answer to this question is to make disciples. For a church to be healthy, and to receive the vision that God has for them to carry out, the church must have a clear response to God's love in their lives. Telling the world, that does not know Him, of this love and how this love has changed our lives, this is the commission of the church. There is no debating, bargaining, or laying aside any part of that mission that Jesus has given us. A church can only be healthy when its members are willing and eager to witness to others. Stetzer and Nation say, "In the Great Commission, Jesus gives a command that is for all churches at all times and in all cultures. It is the missional call for the body of believers in general and individual believers in particular. Each church or group discovers specific ways to respond to its culture, but all churches make that response with certain foundational truths and practices."[2]

> *And Jesus came and spoke to them, saying, "All authority has been given to Me in heaven and on earth. Go therefore and make disciples of all the nations, baptizing them in the name of the Father and of the Son and the Holy Spirit, teaching them to observe all things that I have commanded you; and lo, I am with you always, even to the end of the age." Amen. Matthew 28:18-20*

As we find it in the scriptures in the original Greek language of the New Testament, the word "go" literally means "as you are going." This is saying that we need to be a people prepared daily to carry the message of Jesus Christ to whomever we meet and come in contact with. We are a sent people with a sent purpose. As Christ ambassadors, we do poorly when we try to close ourselves off from other opportunities, and this includes withdrawing ourselves within our church community and shirking back from proclaiming the good news to the community. The church must never lose the sense that we are sent. Staying at home base is not an option that Christ gives us as a church and a church community. We cannot stay within the walls of our church and act like it's an army fort somewhere in the wilderness afraid of savages that will harm us. That is not the case, we are surrounded by people who need us desperately to proclaim the good news to them to help them to see that Christ is the answer and Christ is the salvation from an eternally burning hell. We never know what our presence may mean to another person on a particular day. That may be the day that God has placed us at the crossroads with them, for them to be able to choose because of our witness to them at that moment. Not only is their choice important, but also our choice of whether or not to share the gospel can have eternal consequences for more than just us.

A church that is going through the revitalization process must witness and make disciples, that is not a choice it is an imperative. There cannot be a true revitalization in a church without a church going into the world, seeking those who are lost and in need of Christ to save them.. We cannot pull back and be afraid to proclaim Jesus to the world that needs him. As a church, this is our sole duty, which is to tell the world about Him. We make disciples by intentionally carrying this message to the lost everywhere we go and prepared to proclaim it at every open door and opportunity that is presented before us. Every believer should be known as a missionary going into the world sharing with them the word and the love of Christ.

Living a missionary passion for the lost

Unfortunately, many churches live in a state of reluctance or downright refusal to go into the community and minister to the ones that need it the most. It seems that in the culture we live in today that it is becoming more and more the case that churches are shutting in on themselves and shutting the world out. When in fact we are told to go out into the world and to preach the gospel to everyone and all nations. We all know very well the story of Jonah, ever since our earliest days in Sunday school class the sermon points of our preacher's message about reluctance. We need to examine ourselves and consider whether we are like Jonah? Are we reluctant to share the gospel of God's message of repentance out of our fear, or anger to those outside of our faith, or for other reasons that are not spoken to anyone else? Do we even care about the lost? Do we go as Jonah did and hide under a leaf and complain about these miserable people that God has placed before me? Are we willing to let God demonstrate His love through us to the people that do not know Him?

In answer to God's call to missional living, we must decide whom we serve and recognize what our motives are within us. And we need to examine our hearts and determine those motivations which should be the love of Christ in us, and that we want to share this with others. Before a church can be a witnessing church to the world outside the church must have its heart in right alignment with God before that witness can be effective and produce the desired result. Paul tells us, *"Examine yourselves as to whether you are in the faith. Test yourselves. Do you not know yourselves, that Jesus Christ is in you? unless indeed you are disqualified"* (*2 Corinthians 13:5*).

I would also say that we need to know that we are in the right alignment with God's vision and mission for our church and our community. If our hearts are not aligned as they should be, we cannot carry out the mission with the full effectiveness that God desires. Jonah is a perfect example of a wrong heart condition. Jonah had a burning, white-hot emotion of anger in his very soul for these people of Nineveh. When Jonah fled from his Nineveh assignment not because he feared the people but in knowing God might save them and that angered him. The Assyrians were wicked people who were unworthy of redemption; And in the eyes of someone like Jonah, these people were beyond the reach of grace and did not deserve the grace that God was willing and desired to give them. We must make sure that we don't have the same judgmental and anger about people that do not look like us or act like us.

When we are witnessing, we need to have a heart like God which is a heart that is compassionate and full of love because God is love. We need to have a heart that is caring and full of grace. Forgiving and slow to anger, a rich and faithful love. A heart that is willing to redeem and restore. Most importantly, we need to have the fire of God burning in us for the lost. The most frequent reason that churches are not more than smoldering embers is that they do not burn for the lost any longer.

Ready to give an account

> *"But sanctify the Lord God in your hearts, and always be ready*
> *to give a defense to everyone who asks you a reason for the hope*
> *that is in you, with meekness and fear; having a good conscience,*
> *that when they defame you as evildoers, those who revile your*
> *good conduct in Christ may be ashamed." (1 Peter 3:15-16)*

It is amazing but some people just are automatic machines of proclaiming the gospel to anyone and everyone they come in contact with. It does not matter if they're shopping for groceries, going to the laundromat, stopping in at a restaurant, or just walking through a checkout line. They can strike up conversations with people about the gospel of Jesus Christ at a moment's notice. These people are amazing, and we see them, and we admire their confidence, their boldness, and their due diligence in proclaiming the good news.

But I must be honest, that is not easy for most of us. Most of us do not find or have that boldness and courage that comes with proclaiming the gospel like this to others. For many of us, it's like pulling teeth to drum up the courage to have these conversations. So how are we able to talk about Jesus in our everyday lives? If church and mission are more than an event to which we invite people if we are about ordinary life with gospel intentionality, how do we do everyday evangelism and witnessing with others?[3]

Train and practice

We need to train and practice as in any other thing in our life. We cannot assume and believe that we can just walk up to someone and be able to witness and tell someone about the gospel of Jesus Christ without first practicing it effectively, efficiently, and precisely. It is a good idea to talk with your ministry leader whether it be your pastor, associate pastor, Sunday school teacher, or church leadership, and practice telling your story and God's story and how God changed your story through His love. Anyone that plays any type of sports or has any particular skill in their career field knows that it is imperative that practice brings about the wanted and desired results. Think of your Christian friends as your practice partners. Because you will find if it is hard to talk about Jesus with your Christian friends, then how will you expect to talk about Jesus with unbelievers? Getting into the habit of talking about Jesus in your everyday life will help you to train your mind, heart, and soul for the proclamation of the gospel with others more easily and with less consciousness of thought. The goal is to make it second nature to be able to talk about Jesus whether you're with someone as a non-believer or with anyone in normal conversation. Let your unbelieving friends over here have conversations with your fellow Christians about Jesus. Even include them in the conversation more ideally. These opportunities will open doors for you to be able to include them in the conversation and to let them feel more comfortable about participating.

Be patient

We need to be patient and let God be God. Many times, we feel that we must direct, push, and drive the conversation toward God. If we allow God to do His sovereign work in and through us, He will create the opportunities for us to spread the gospel, we do not have to force it. Our responsibility is to move people from one step to another step along the way rather than get them to salvation immediately. It can happen immediately but that is only because God has already been working in that person ahead of time before we even opened our mouths. But more times, it is more likely that it is a relationship-building process for many non-believers. We live in a post-Christian culture where people want to see God in you and in your life rather than just being told. God still draws people unto Him, but the world is not like it was even 50 years ago.

Sometimes less is more. We often find when we are sharing the gospel alongside someone else that we wish they would shut up and not say so much. They seem desperate to convince or persuade the person into salvation right then, when in fact it is a step-by-step process many times with many listeners. We need to give people time to think and let the Holy

Spirit do His work in them. Give them a chance to think before you unload another heap of strange ideas to them that they do not understand. Trust in the Holy Spirit to work on their hearts and in their lives. The Holy Spirit is the ultimate evangelist. The Holy Spirit is the one that persuades people of the truth. He convicts them of sin, righteousness, and judgment. Our job is to present the gospel, it is His job to save.

Keep it simple stupid

When we find ourselves in opportunities to present the gospel to someone, we tend to unload too much information upon the hearer to absorb all at one time. If we used a scale from 1 to 10 where people are in their spiritual knowledge and the rate of absorption of the information, we tend to give people the information as if they were 8 and 9's when in fact they may be 1 and 2's. We often tend to overcomplicate things. Some cannot help themselves but want to explain redemption, sanctification, and regeneration in the first part of a conversation with someone that may not have any church background or church experience at all in their life. These people mean well and they're trying to give all the information they can to the people so that they can be informed but that is not what they're needing at that point. A good way of walking someone through the need for salvation without getting into too many complicated theological assumptions is to talk about creation, the fall, redemption, and restoration. In this way, you can touch on their identity, the problem, the solution, and the hope that Jesus Christ has for them and salvation.

Proclaiming the truths of God

All unbelievers have certain insecurities and fears in their life that they deal with daily. These fears and insecurities are a fact whether they acknowledge that fact or not. We know that every person is broken and hurting in some way or another. By proclaiming the truth of God, we can give them the truth and speak into their insecurities and fears. Think about people you know that are busy, stressed out, and worn out in their lives and don't seem to have time for God. Take a moment to examine how a failure to believe one or more of the truths of God can be the root cause of why they struggle with a relationship with God.

1. **God is great, so we don't have to be in control.** They might be too busy because they are insecure and need to control life, when in fact, God is great and cares for us as a sovereign heavenly Father.

2. **God is glorious, so we don't have to fear others.** They might be struggling because they fear other people and cannot say no to them, but when God is gracious, and his opinion is the one that matters, fear will fall away.

3. **God is good, so we don't have to look somewhere else.** They might be too worn out because they are filling their lives with activity in a desperate attempt to find satisfaction, but God is good and the true source of joy for us and fills us with that joy.

4. **God is gracious, so we don't have to prove anything ourselves.** They might be too stressed because they are trying to prove themselves through their work, but God is gracious and justifies us freely through faith in the finished work of Jesus Christ.

So, every one of these truths is the good news. As we talk with people, you can ask yourself which of these four truths they are failing to believe in themselves. Then you can begin to think about how you can speak this truth into their lives and into their situations.

Ask simple questions

When in conversation with non-believers we need to keep in mind that simple but powerful questions can make all the difference in opening the door for witnessing and evangelism. Instead of trying to push your way into a conversation about Jesus, try having a normal conversation with the non-believer and ask simple questions to "why" or "why does it matter so much to you" or even a question of "what do you want?", can lead into conversations about Christ. We can take these questions and the subjects that they are talking about and relate them to the four truths about God. You can steer the conversation to spiritual things. This gives you an opportunity you can speak into their lives, speak the truth of God into their lives and help them to start to think and ponder the things that are spiritual and the eternal things. Michael Frost in his book "Surprised the World the five habits of highly missional people" says, "that we need to be living questionable lives."[4] We need to be living our lives in such a way that people want to ask us why we do, why we say, why we act the way we do? And that gives us a chance to tell them about Jesus and how Jesus saved our lives and has turned us around and made us new creatures in Him. This is the practice of witnessing and witnessing well for Jesus.

When a church is in the process of revitalization and is promoting and exhibiting the lifestyle of witnessing and evangelism, that church is healthier and more passionate about reaching lost people everywhere. Nina Gunter, a long-time director and supporter of Nazarene Missions International and General Superintendent Emeritus, says that "if you take missions out of the Bible you would only have the leather cover left." This is about as it can be. As a people of God, we need the Bible as a missionary book and not just good rules and guidelines to go by. The Bible should be our road map, our instructions for being witnesses to everyone around the nation. The church needs to be a place that models mission passion with every breath that we take and everything that we do. The church is about building the Kingdom of God and expanding the stakes on the tent of God.

Telling our Story

Many churches say that they are identified as loving churches. That people that come talk about how much they love each other. The church I pastor is no different than most others. I have heard the statement by several in the church, especially in the early days, that we are a loving church. The response that I automatically wanted to blurt back to them was, yes, you're a loving church but you love the ones that are in your group and the ones that are in the church. But if anyone comes in that they do not know or is outside of that circle they shun them and don't even approach them. So, the question must be, where is the love that you're talking about?

Since I became Pastor, our church has had more heart for the people in the community that does not know Jesus. But it was not easy, and it was not all of a sudden or something that became natural for them. It took time. It takes time for people that are so used to their ways for so many years to be able to have their mindset and their heart set changed in such a way that it becomes part of them. Many things had to happen for us to be able to do that. For a long time, it seemed like we "did ministry", and we were doing it well, but God was prompting my heart and convicting me that we were doing ministry "OK", but were we building the Kingdom? When we were handing out food in our weekly food distribution, were we just handing them more groceries, or were we giving them hope and speaking love and light into them that is from Jesus? Were we making a difference in their lives by handing them boxes of food? Were we giving them hope when they felt like they had no hope? These questions and more are what we had to look at. Questioning whether we were going through the motions of doing things and asking why were we doing things? And because of that, as we changed how we do our food distribution. Iif someone needs prayer, or we hear of a situation that needs prayer and they request, we will stop everything we are doing and go to their car, or go to where they are and we will pray with them, pray over them, pray for them regardless of how many people are in line or how many people are waiting.

We ask simple questions. Many times, as I get a food box together for someone, or I help them with clothes or other items they may need I ask follow up questions, very simple, how is your relationship with God? Or how has your relationship been with God lately? And many times, I get answers that are vague and roundabout and beat around the bush. It opens the door for me to speak into their life and tell them the truth. Most of them already know the truth and they just want to try to deny it or avoid it, but our job is to let them know that there is hope and that there is help and that there is someone that loves them so much that He died for them and took their place. These are the eternal things that matter. And when it's all said and done that's the only thing that matters.

Reflection questions

1. Are we all evangelists? Do you know anyone who is gifted as an evangelist?
2. Do you feel pressure as a Christian to act as an evangelist? In what ways do you most typically share your faith with or demonstrate it to your friends and neighbors?
3. What measures can you take in your church to help you and your other fellow church members to become better witnesses for Jesus Christ?

Best practices and ideas

1. Practice talking to trusted fellow Christians and talk about Jesus with them.
2. When talking to non-believers, be patient and realize that their knowledge and their experiences will probably not be like yours.
3. Ask simple questions that will prompt a conversation about the spiritual wellness of the person that you are talking with.
4. Proclaim the truth of God and let your foundation be built upon those in your conversation and your witnessing.

CHAPTER 11

Putting Actions to Your Words Successfully

But be doers of the word, and not hearers only,
deceiving yourselves. (James 1:22)

But do you want to know, O foolish man, that faith
without works is dead? (James 2:20)

There are some things in life that you can just jump into with both feet. You can take the plunge and just go for the gusto. Those things are alright if you're going to jump in an icy lake to go swimming or take a weekend adventure with your buddies. But it is not a good idea for churches, especially churches that are in the process of revitalization, to just jump in with both feet and to just start doing things without plans. To be quite honest, that is the quickest way to fail. When leading a church in the revitalization process there must be a vision, mission, strategy, and financing that must be accomplished by doing successful and meaningful ministry in the church. There is no room for jumping in without thinking about the cost and the consequences in the first place. Jesus himself says, "For which of you, intending to build a tower, does not sit down first and count the cost, whether he has enough to finish it" (Luke 14:28).

I had talked about how we planned and prepared for the new ministry of NazKids for our church. We spent many weeks figuring out the location of the ministry to start, how we would do the service, and who would be the primary leaders for NazKids. Although a couple of voices spoke up and asked why we had to plan so much, most understood the importance of doing it well. There comes a time when all the planning does need to move into action.

NazKids was a direct result of the church survey that was filled out early in my pastorate at the church. Many of the responders to the question of what the most important thing for the church was to do, was get more children and families in the church. This was an answer to how it would be accomplished. Instead of trying to get kids to come to the church, the church would go to them. We had to think outside the box. Churches needing revitalization must push outside the envelope of their normal thinking. Change the way they have always thought. If they continue to do the same thing over and over, they will end up with the same old results.

For a church to do revitalization well, there needs to be careful thought, discussion and planning with all the leadership and the congregation of the church. Because you need all the church to participate and to be part of the success of the ministry. You can not expect to have fire in the church without some sort of building of that flame. There are steps to building a sustainable fire in the church, the same principles as building any other fire. Consider the following key elements to putting action to your words and plans in the revitalization process.

Keys to Successful Action Ministry

1. **Take command.** As we have talked about throughout this book, there are some severe and critical things that the church has been through and will continue to go through during the revitalization process. And if the only thing we looked at was the despair and seemingly hopelessness that the church may be experiencing at this moment then we would be depressed and discouraged from trying to do anything further. but as someone had said long ago, we need to pull ourselves up by the bootstraps. Leadership especially revitalization leadership, cannot dwell in the past. But leadership must see what God intends and what God wants through the vision and take command of the situation.

This requires leadership that has been prayed up and read up, listening to God for what he wants for his church. And to have the gumption and the stamina and the strength to continue leading forward for that revitalization. Using Paul as an example, leaders need to be willing to bring kindling to the fire to grow and fuel it.

2. **Lead by example.** It is good to lead but it is better to lead by example. The people we are leading need to see that the leader is invested in this process. That the leader has a stake in the outcome of the revitalization effort. That the leader has the same heart and same love for this church and is willing to sacrifice and put sweat equity into the effort. They need to see that we are willing to go collect the fodder for the fire and invest in the success of the church. A leader that just points fingers and gives commands to people to do things will not get the respect and the needed effort of the people that surround him or her. Jesus is our perfect example of how to be an example. He was willing, the King of creation, to stoop down and wash the dirty feet of His disciples. He was willing to humble Himself and to take care of their needs before He took care of His.

3. **Listen aggressively.** The importance of listening to leadership is crucial for team performance. A leader who is authoritarian and judgmental may cause their people to be hesitant and unwilling to communicate. This can lead to team dysfunction and poor productivity. So why are listening skills important? Here are ways that listening skills make you a more effective leader: Listening increases your capacity as a leader. We can always learn from those around us. Effective listening gives you knowledge and perspectives that increase your leadership capacity. Being open to feedback and new ideas from your staff/volunteers helps you learn and grow as a leader.

Listening shows you care. Listening to someone shows you care about what they're saying and empathize with their feelings. This creates a work environment of trust. Having the trust of your leaders and people gives you greater influence over them. At the same time, it makes them more motivated and committed to their work. Listening helps you comprehend the situation. If you fail to pay due attention to what your people say, you will not fully understand the situation. Failing to comprehend the situation may lead you to give advice or recommendations that are ineffective or don't get to the root of the problem. Listening helps you better understand your context. Listening to others is the best way to understand the needs of your congregants and church. This helps you plan effective strategies that are oriented to the demands of your church's ministries. Listening gives you a vision of reality on the ground. Listening gives you knowledge and insights into the day-to-day reality of your co-ministry leaders. It's essential to create an atmosphere of trust and encourage your staff/volunteers to speak openly about their ministry challenges. You might be surprised at how different their reality is from your perception of it.[1]

1. **Communicate purpose and meaning.** Not only is listening well a critical skill but communicating the vision and mission is essential. Understand why you are communicating and what you want to accomplish by delivering your message. Communication serves five major purposes: to inform, express feelings, imagine, influence, and meet social expectations. Each of these purposes is reflected in a form of communication. How we communicate can mean success or failure. Relevant information must flow continuously from top to bottom and vice versa. Communicate your message as directly and concisely as possible. Be sure to offer appropriate background so that your audience understands the context of the message, but do not overwhelm them with irrelevant information. The staff at all levels must be kept informed about the church's objectives and other developments taking place in the ministries being overseen. The communication facilitates flow of information, ideas, beliefs, perception, advice, opinion, orders, and instructions. Proper and effective communication is an important tool in the hands of the leadership of any church to bring about an overall change in the revitalization effort.

2. **Create a climate of trust.** It has been said about leadership, that, "if no one is following you then you are just on a walk." Trust is

the biggest thing about leading others. Trust is not assigned but earned. Leaders that lead well build relationships with others. They do not have to be intimate relationships, but relationships that demonstrate your character, integrity, and motives. Character is the quality that lets people feel comfortable about how they will react to certain situations as they arise. Character is the spirit of a person that people are drawn to and admire. Integrity is still doing the right thing even when no one else is looking. People trust that you are, who you say you are, at all times regardless. Motives are the driving force behind your actions and decisions. For revitalizers, the purpose and motive are to advance the Kingdom of God and nothing more. That the leader is taking the most effective and direct route to that goal and purpose. When a leader has these qualities then people trusting and following them is less of a challenge and people will follow with confidence and assurance.

3. **Look for results, not salutes.** Some people can get the results that you are looking for in your ministry efforts. Sometimes the cost is too high. What I mean by this is, that there are times when leaders may be getting some of the results that you are looking for in your ministry, but self-promoting, self-exalting, and self-centeredness can get in the way and taint the results that you received. Some leaders are in a leadership position because they are seeking some type of higher position or using this ministry assignment as a steppingstone to the next best thing. there are times that we need to take caution in having success in ministry. Success can taint a leader that has good intentions from the very beginning, but because of numbers getting better, finances coming in supporting the mission, accolades from peers, and recognition from church leadership can cause a leader to turn from the original intent. They can start seeing and thinking of themselves more highly than they should. Success in ministry needs to be tempered by humility and having a servant's heart. Success can be a dangerous thing if not handled correctly. Success can take your eye off the prize and goal. Paul says that he ran the race with his eye on the prize the whole

time and that he strained for the finish line. "I have fought the good fight, I have finished the race, I have kept the faith" (2 Timothy 4:7). We are also reminded, "Therefore, since we are surrounded by such a great cloud of witnesses, let us throw off everything that hinders and the sin that so easily entangles. And let us run with perseverance the race marked out for us" (Hebrews 12:1).

4. **Take calculated risks.** Taking Risks in Ministry. A leap of faith can lead to great results or failure. In ministry, God calls us to take risks sometimes. That doesn't mean we are careless with finances, reckless with resources, or impulsive with our team. It does mean that we might throw caution to the wind, taking a shot at a big reward over advice to play it safe. When we do take risks, we must be willing to assume the loss. Jesus spoke of the importance of counting the costs, whether it be building a tower (Luke 14:28-30) or going to battle (Luke 14:31-32). There is great wisdom in knowing what you will lose before leaping. Revitalizing churches can also take risks, perhaps by sponsoring a parent-affiliated church, or taking on a staff member with lots of promise but little experience. Pastors who feel led to make a turnaround risk alienating current members for the sake of growing their churches. And building programs are full of risks, even for the healthiest of givers. The most important thing when it comes to risk is knowing what the Lord wants. If you feel Him calling you to take a risk, there's no other move that's safer. When you hear His voice telling you to jump, you should be limber enough to make the move and risk it all.[2]

5. **Go beyond standard procedure.** Whether you realize it or not what you have always done is probably the very thing that got you where you're at now. The need for revitalizing is generally a result of staying the course with ministry choices even when it was obvious that some different choices needed to be made. "We have always done it this way and by golly, we are staying this way." Really? Even when it doesn't work anymore! I know that we have been talking about staying on the old paths, but that is the path of foundational in Jesus' teaching and established biblical way.

But as we refer to methods of ministry, we need to see the way of delivery as open to change. Ready to adjust how we deliver and not what we deliver. As a revitalization leader, you need to be able to go beyond the standard procedure of the way of doing things and be open to thinking outside the box. We serve a God that thinks outside the box. When needed God splits seas, He brings water out of rocks, raises people from the dead, and brings salvation to mankind through a cruel rugged cross. Thinking outside the box is God's MO.

6. **Generate unity.** A good revitalization leader brings about unity among the church team that he is working with. One of the most important responsibilities of a leader is to promote team unity. This does not mean that there are no disagreements or even periodic conflicts on the team or within the church. To be a unifier, the leader brings people together around a vision, a mission, or a project. Team unity drives results. The main objective of a leader is to move a group of people from point A to point B in an as effective way as possible. American poet Mattie Stepanek once said, "Unity is strength…when there is teamwork and collaboration, wonderful things can be achieved." A captain of any sailing ship can point the ship in the right direction, but it takes the whole crew to get the ship to the desired destination in a unified effort. Leaders without the team helping you to achieve the goal you're not going to make it where you want to be.

Action Is the Greatest Need

Many are the needs of our day…The need for peace in war-torn areas around the world. The need for food and clothing in our poverty-stricken communities and countries around the world. The need for loving families, civil rights, good-paying jobs, etc.

These needs are certainly noble and very important, yet I suggest that the greatest need for our world is for the church to not only talk about our needs in committees and board meetings but to go and put hands and feet to our words with evangelism. Sharing the gospel with every person (Mk 16:15). Preaching the word everywhere (Ac 8:5). A need that was met aggressively in the first century Church (Col 1:23). Why evangelism is "The Greatest Need" may not be apparent to some, so a reminder of why the need is so great.

The Condition of the World.

Billions are dying, lost in sin! For all have sinned (Ro 3:23). Knowing that without Jesus, they will die in their sins (Jn 8:24). What does this mean close to home to us? It means that relatives, friends, and neighbors will be lost without ever receiving an opportunity from you to hear the gospel message. Many Christians are doing little if anything to teach them. So, what does this mean in nations far away? Precious souls will die outside of Christ. Because many Christians are unwilling to either go or send (Ro 10:14-15). Unless we do something to meet this need, souls will be lost!

The Condition of the Church.

Many congregations have lost their focus. They have become little more than a social club. Meeting only the social and emotional needs of its members. They have become burdened by that which is the responsibility of others (1Ti 5:16). Many congregations are declining in number. As Christians die or fall away, little is being done to convert others. Where numerical growth occurs, it is often by Christians moving into the area. Unless we do something to meet this need, many churches will cease to exist!

So, the need is great, for to save others and to save ourselves we need to put our plans into action and move out and serve and evangelize! Yet consider why the need is not being met. For some, it is a lack of concern. Not concerned for the Lord's cause, who came to seek and save those who were lost (Luke 19:10). Not concerned for those lost and dying in sin, unlike Paul (Romans 10:1). Not concerned for their welfare, endangered by failing to bear fruit (John 15:1-2). Have we become so hardened, that we no longer care?

For Some, It Is a Lack of Knowledge.

Lacking knowledge of God's word. Perhaps unaware that Jesus calls us to this mission (Matthew 28:19). Perhaps needing to be taught again so we may teach others (Hebrews 5:12). Lacking knowledge of what to do, and what to say. When it can often be as simple as saying, "come and see" (John 1:45-46). When it simply involves sharing with others what you have believed and done. Are we willing to make the effort to learn, so that others might be saved?

For Some, It Is a Lack of Courage.

There is a fear of being rejected by loved ones, ridiculed by friends and strangers, and reviled by enemies of Christ. Yet there is no need to fear such things. People are not rejecting us, but Christ. If we are reviled for the name of Christ, we are blessed (Matthew 5:11-12). If we are servants of Christ, we seek to please God, not men (Galatians 1:10). Are we willing to overcome our fears, to save those who are lost?

For Some, It Is a Lack of Faith.

It is a lack of faith because they don't believe that God's word is true. When it describes the simple condition of the world (Romans 3:23). When it describes the terrible consequences of sin (Romans 6:23). Who doesn't believe in the ability of God Himself? to give them the strength to do God's will (Philippians 4:13). To give them the wisdom to teach His word (James 1:5). To give them the courage to share His will (2 Timothy 1:7-8). Are we willing to have the faith to trust in God that others might be saved?

For Some, It Is a Lack of Focus.

They lack focus because they are distracted by things in the world. these distractions stifle our efforts to bear fruit (Luke 8:14). These distractions also make one unprepared for the day of the Lord (Luke 21:34). They are trying to do the impossible such as serving two masters (Luke 16:13). They are trying to love both the Father and the world (1 John 2:15-17). I suspect this is the major reason why people don't evangelize today and go and put their words into action. the question is are we willing to seek first the Kingdom of God, making its growth our priority?

Whatever the reason for "The Greatest Need" not being met, there is no excuse. To encourage us to meet this need, consider some reasons.

Why We All Need to Be Workers

We all need to be workers to fulfill the commandment of Christ. Jesus commanded that we make disciples (Matthew 28:19). Disciples who are taught to observe what he commanded (Matthew 28:20). The Great Commission is not fulfilled until we are making disciples!

We are to be workers to show our love for others. Love for others was the second greatest command of the Old Testament (Matthew 22:39). Love for one another is debt that can never be fully paid (Romans 13:8). We are to love even our enemies (Matthew 5:44-45). What greater love can we show, than to offer others the way of salvation?

We all need to be workers to be like the early church. To be the Lord's church, we must follow the pattern of the Church of Acts. To be the Lord's church, we must also demonstrate the same zeal for the Lord's work and love for the last. Unless we restore the spirit and soul of New Testament Christianity, we are only a skeleton!

We should also be workers in the field because of the fear of the Lord. To fear God serves to motivate the apostle Paul (2 Corinthians 5:10-11). Jesus spoke much about souls being lost (Matthew 7:13) and in (Mark 16:16). The reality of Judgement Day and souls lost should move us to the action!

The greatest need of the church is to get back to its original mission. The greatest need of Christians is to be personal workers in the vineyard of the Lord. The current apathy and rate of decline in many churches are revealing. It reveals that there has been a lack of concern, knowledge, courage, faith, and focus. That this lack has hindered the most important work of the church.

What can we do?

To ask that question indicates concern, that is good!

To the one asking they need to add knowledge and learn!

To knowledge, one needs to add courage and pray!

Then with faith and focus, we can work together to fulfill "The Greatest Need"[3]

Telling our Story

The founding pastor was the one that propelled the church forward for 4 decades. He was the driving force behind most of the advancement of the Kingdom in this congregation. Except for one or two others, he was the fire that sustained the church. To this day, many talks about how he was a go-getter. Always pushing forward, trying to advance the Kingdom at every opportunity that he had. The strange thing to me is that they never talk about how any of them were the ones on fire for the mission of God.

Since most of the growth and development of the church came from the founding pastor, after his death the church was stuck in place, not knowing which way to turn. They had no idea how to move the church or to keep the fire burning that he had done for so many years. They were stuck in a time capsule, frozen in the point of time at his death. The action had stopped, and they were declining and dying at an accelerated rate of speed. It is now or never for this small congregation.

The flame had to be fanned again for the congregation and the church ministries. Visions had to be put into action and there was not much time to waste. A breakthrough for us was the implementation of the Shepherd's Pantry in the parking lot of our church. The idea came from the concept of the little library boxes that are all around the country, where people put in books to share with anyone around the community to read and share again. For Shepherd's Pantry boxes it was food instead. The motto was "Give what you can, take what you need." The Shepherd's Pantry is a grassroots, community-sourced solution to immediate and local needs. Whether a need for food or a need to give, Shepherd's Pantry facilitates neighbors helping neighbors, and building community. The Shepherd's Pantry utilizes a familiar, compelling concept to pique local interest in and action against local food insecurity. The Shepherd's Pantry offers a place around which neighbors might come together to meet neighborhood needs, whether for food or other basic needs.

How does Shepherd's Pantry create action on the part of your church and individually? Many food pantries require an application process before use and have set hours of operation. Anyone may access Shepherd's Pantry at any time. Food pantries operate as service providers, those who use them as clients. These pantries dissolve that professional boundary. Whether stocking or taking stock, everyone approaches The Shepherd's Pantry the same way, mediating the shame that accompanies need. Traditional pantries are critical in addressing food insecurity. But some people can fall through the cracks. The Shepherd's Pantry is a safety net. The pantries are a proving ground, testing concepts like community, charity, justice, and sharing economy. A tremendous advantage of the panties is that they are open 24/7, no questions asked, The Shepherd's Pantry fills gaps in service provided by organizations with operating hours and/or required paperwork/documentation. It also encourages community and love for neighbors. The Shepherd's Pantry does not come with performance metrics or guarantees but is a leap of faith in people. This is a good example of putting concepts into action. Examples like this show that even the smallest steps to obedience can lead to blessing and Kingdom impact to the point of unimaginable limits. A person that saw the posting on social media about the Shepherd's Pantry said this, "Pastor Rob Beckett - You and your church have lit a fire in our community! Not only are you excited to open it, but our community is excited to participate! Well done! Now Shepherdsville... Let's take it to the next level!"

You never know what might be the spark that ignites a fire in your church and, in the case of the pantries, in the community. The point is this, action, the action makes it all happen. Another way of stating it is obedience to what God has shown you. When God places a vision in you there must be action and obedience to carry that vision to fruition.

Reflection Questions

1. Does your leadership and church members have the faith to step out and put your words to action?
2. Does your church leadership have the right focus?
3. Does your church even care about others that are outside the church? If you do, then are you doing anything about it?

Best Practices/Ideas

1. Take a community assessment and see what needs are in your community and see how your church can get involved in them.
2. Speak to community leaders and see where they could use the assistance and volunteers in your community.
3. Reach out to school resource personnel and see how your church can get involved.
4. The main thing is to get out in the community and don't just complain about it. Be the change.

CHAPTER 12

Effectiveness is Not Defined By Size

*"And whatever you do, do it heartily, as to the Lord and
not to men, knowing that from the Lord you will receive the
reward of the inheritance; for you serve the Lord Christ."*
(Colossians 3:23-24)

I 'm glad David was not deterred by the size of the giant. I'm glad Gideon
was not scared off from the battle because of a handful of men. I'm glad
the early church did not allow their smallness to keep them from being
world changers. And I'm glad that you are not letting your size stop you
from doing Kingdom work. The truth is, God doesn't ask us to be bigger
than we are but to be true to who He calls us to be for His Kingdom.
Small churches must know that God has a plan for them that far exceeds
anything they can imagine or dream.

*"For the Lord does not see as man sees; for man looks at the outward
appearance, but the Lord looks at the heart" (1 Samuel 16:7b).*

In the Kingdom of God, everyone who is invited is capable of serving
and is not insubstantial or insignificant. Why is it that the first thing
we often think about when it comes to church growth is the size of our
congregation? The truth is, it doesn't matter if we have a hundred members
or a thousand, if we are being faithful to what God has called us to do, then
we are making an impact on His Kingdom. So don't be discouraged if your

church is small. Remember that God sees your heart and He knows your potential. He will use you in ways that you never could have imagined, to reach people for His Kingdom.

What if we had churches with David's heart?

Little man syndrome definition: A man, small in stature, who attempts to overcome the way he believes other people perceive him by attaching himself to authority figures, trying to manipulate himself into positions of control, gravitating toward positions of leadership, and having a fairly volatile temper. I had a boss with little man syndrome and besides never being able to please him, he always had to prove he was better than anyone else!

David, although being the youngest of all his brothers never demonstrated these traits in his character. As we know, David was a man after God's own heart. There are many lessons that we can learn from David for the small church today. Even before he was ever crowned King of Israel, he demonstrated qualities and characteristics that serve us well in our time now.

Churches can get caught up in a little congregation syndrome of their own if not careful. God doesn't ask them to be bigger than they are but to be true to who He calls them to be for the Kingdom. Small churches must know that God has a plan for them that far exceeds anything that they can imagine or dream.

In God's economy, everyone that is called is qualified for service in His Kingdom and they are not insignificant or too small. Why is it that the first thing people ask when you mention your church is "how many people go to your church?" It's because we use a matrix of measurement that does not say anything about the success or effectiveness of the congregation. We know that whom God calls, He also equips. *1 Samuel 16:13 "Then Samuel took the horn of oil and anointed him amid his brothers, and the Spirit of the Lord came upon David from that day forward."*

Next, a church with David's heart serves at his father's command. *1 Samuel 16:20 And Jesse took a donkey loaded with bread, a skin of wine, and a young goat, and sent them by his son David to Saul.* David was an obedient and faithful servant. He was obedient to his father to serve the needs of his brothers. Churches with David's heart will serve the needs of others in the church family and the surrounding community. Jesus set the example for the church by coming to serve and not to be served.

Also, another characteristic of David's heart is the intolerance of harassment and taunting of the enemy without retaliation. *1 Samuel 17:32 Then David said to Saul, "Let no man's heart fail because of him; your servant will go and fight with this Philistine."* When David heard the clamoring and jeering from the Philistines, he could not sit still for it. He knew action had to be taken. Churches today need to be the same when the enemy is taunting and causing trouble. Troubles need to be addressed immediately with prayer, guidance from God, and action on the leadership's part before it becomes a standoff where everyone sees the problem, but no one is willing to move because of fear.

"So, Saul clothed David with his armor, and he put a bronze helmet on his head; he also clothed him with a coat of mail. David fastened his sword to his armor and tried to walk, for he had not tested them." And David said to Saul, "I cannot walk with these, for I have not tested them." So, David took them off" (1 Samuel 17:38-39). Churches today are trying to wear the armor of another church that does not fit them. The tendency is to see another church do something and get positive results and think that they can just do the same things with equal outcomes. This is not always the case, and each congregation needs to understand that their context may have a different situation compared to other churches. Go into battle with the armor that God has given you, even if it is only a sling and a stone. We know the rest of the story, that David slew the mighty giant. Small churches with David's hearts are capable of slaying their giants as well.

"Lord, This Is All I've Got" (2 Kings 4:2, Luke 21:1-4)

It was a sad day; it was a hopeless day for the widow. The creditors had come to claim the defenseless widow's two sons, for payment of a debt that her late husband had occurred. She had no assets, no payment to offer in substitution for her sons except a pot of oil. "Lord, this is all I've got." But that pot of oil was the foundation, the start of a fortune that saved the boys from slavery and the family from bankruptcy. A little oil and a handful of meals provided food for the prophet and the widow for a whole year.

Another widow, Jesus observed giving two mites. This was everything that was in her bank account and pockets. Others were giving a little bit off the top of their abundance. They were peeling just a couple of bills off the roll that they had wrapped in rubber bands. She was willing to say, "Lord, this is all that I've got"

A petrified army frozen in their tracks for days was shaken and freed by a shepherd lad that brought deliverance to a nation stalemated by the challenges of Goliath. He went suited only with a sling and a stone. "Lord, this is all I've got.

A little boy's lunch of 5 loaves and 2 fish provided food for ten thousand hungry people in the desert. "Lord, this is all I've got"

Three hundred followers of Gideon put to flight an army that was four hundred to one against them. "The Lord said, this is all I want."

Who then can say that the small and insignificant things do not count and are of no use? It seems that it is insignificant that God blesses, and if God blesses, then it is no longer insignificant.

In Judges Chapter 7 the army of Gideon started with 32,000 men. The Midianites had 120,000 men. Talk about feeling the pressure. But God looked and saw that the odds were too uneven, so He told Gideon to reduce the number of men he had. I'm sure Gideon, although a faithful warrior, thought this is crazy. But he did as God said, and the soldiers were taken down to 10,000 men. Then God looked again, and said, too many men Gideon, and the number was reduced to 300 men. God looked and said, this is just right, now stand back and watch. We know who won the battle.

Any small congregation can be noticed by God and take the lead in their community. You may be small in number, but you can win big battles for the Lord in your community. You don't have to be a mega or even a large church to see a real and evident change in the community that you live in. God may be looking and saying that before I send you a bunch of people you must trust in me. You get too big too quick you might start getting the big head and start forgetting who is the commander of the battles. But it takes people that have hearts and courage to fight and are ready and willing that are on the alert for the battles that face you. "Little is much when God is in it."

The Shepherds sling (1 Samuel 17)

We have heard the story over and over since our youth. We know how God used a young and scrawny boy, compared to Goliath, to kill and defeat the enemy. We had already talked about having David's heart but let's look at what the young boy used, a simple and unadvanced weapon to fend off animals and pests. The sling was not a conventional weapon for warfare. But this was what David was accustomed to using and it worked for him. You cannot effectively wear someone else's armor. Saul tried to place his armor on David, but it did not fit.

There are some things that your church has done before that may not fit now. The church must not cower down to the taunting of the world that we live in, we have to be willing to take the tools and the weapons that we are fitted to and use them so God can achieve His purpose and will. The church in which you serve needs to look at the tools and weapons that God has equipped you with and use those to the Glory of God. He has allowed you to be a small and or rural church for a reason, use it to the fullest of your extent. We look around in the neighborhood and we say this is bad and that is wrong. I've never seen things like this before. Chances are that your church can be the answer and solution to some of the things that are wrong and broken in your community. "Little is much when God is in it."

The Boy's lunch (John 6:1-13)

Jesus came into town, and everyone turned out to see Him because everybody was talking about all the things He had been doing. Knowing it was time for the disciples to have another lesson, He asked Phillip how they would feed all the people that had gathered. Andrew remembered seeing a boy with lunch, so he took the boy to see Jesus. He took the food, gave thanks, and gave it to them. The more they passed out the more they had. Five fishes and two loaves became 12 baskets of leftovers. "Little is much when God is in it."

Compared and measured against the size of the crowd and the size of the need, the lunch was not much. But Jesus, God in flesh, saw the need and had compassion. He was moved to act. He had to do something. We know the story; He told the disciples to pass it out and they kept passing out more and more.

Do you want to earn the right to speak into other people's lives about the saving power and redeeming blood of Christ? Then touch their physical need, ease their hunger pains, and alleviate some of their worries about where the next meal comes from. Jesus, throughout scripture, ate a lot of meals, with a lot of people, at a lot of tables.

The Widows Pot of Oil and The Widow's Mite (2 Kings 4, Luke 21)

The widow with oil and the widow with 2 mites were miracles that were used by God. We understand the oil being a miracle but how are 2 mites given to be a miracle? Philip Brooks suggested that God makes miracles out of His people, rather than using His people to work miracles. The little is enough only when it is all there is and nothing else is left. The widow's 2 mites constituted a treasure worthy of a queen because there was nothing left when these were given.

If the mighty are available, the mighty are chosen. But God uses the instrument that is yielded, and a rod in the hand of Moses becomes a scepter when it is a badge of devotion. God will use the hand of the many if they are ready for battle, but if not, He will use the few. There must not be any holding back. My all is enough for God to work with. Michelangelo said, "Perfection is composed of small, seemingly insignificant things, but perfection is no small or insignificant thing." Full consecration to God is composed of the devotion to little things, but full consecration itself is no little thing. God asked Moses what was in his hand. For Moses, it was a rod, but for God, it was an instrument to split seas. For David, his was a sling for defense from wild animals, but for God, it was a way to deliver a nation by killing a giant. For the little boy, it was a sack lunch, but for Jesus, it was a way of filling the multitude. What's in your hand? Are you like the widow with the oil? pouring all I've got out for God. And are you like the widow with only 2 mites? Giving all I've got to God, complete surrender. "Little is much when God is in it"

"Give all and the best we got"
(Matthew 6:33-34, Colossians 3:23-24)

"And whatever you do, do it heartily, as to the Lord and not to men, knowing that from the Lord you will receive the reward of the inheritance; for you serve the Lord Christ."

Does excellence matter to God? Does God care about quality? Is He concerned with how well things are done? Does it make any difference to God whether: the instruments are in tune; the worship team has rehearsed the songs, etc.? Some would say, "No." All God cares about is our hearts. It's the thought that counts. God is not impressed with a slick program or flashy audio-visuals; what matters to Him are internal things like love, compassion, and humility. That's right – partially, but it's also partially wrong. God doesn't care about those things in and of themselves. God is primarily concerned with our hearts. But God does care about those things as an expression of our hearts. Because the way we serve God in the church, in our homes, in our workplaces, and in our families do matter greatly to God. The way we live out our faith; the level of commitment we have, to doing things well, to honoring God in every area of our lives, are what reveal what is in our hearts. It's not the things themselves God cares about. It's what those things say about our hearts.[1]

The noblest of ambitions in any man tends to measure or define the man. The most important ambition of Paul was to "serve the Lord Christ." His supreme desire was to make others know and serve the Lord.

As for the size of a church, God is concerned with the heart condition rather than how big, or popular a church is. The church is called into a life of courageous service. "Ye serve the Lord Christ" The power of Christ within us is stronger than all other forces that press against us. "Now let me burn out for God!" exclaimed Henry Martyn when he arrived in Calcutta in April 1806. But he probably had little idea how fast the blaze would consume him. He died six years later at the age of 31. Eager to devote his life to the Lord's work in India, with an incredible determination and unselfish dedication, Martyn compressed a lifetime of service into those six years. "I care not what hardships I endure if only I win souls for Christ."[2]

It takes courage to live to your convictions and not bend to the popular opinion of the day. Your courage will find expression in and reveal itself in your service. We are not to be called to be children of luxury and ease but to a life of self-giving and cross-bearing. "Ye serve the Lord Christ" You might say wait a minute, you are trying to talk me into poverty and suffering? NO. I can't talk you into anything, it must be a pure and selfless dedication to the Lord. If it is not from the heart, no amount of work will accomplish anything.

The church is also called into a life of SACRIFICIAL service. The essence of Christ's service is in sacrifice. The sacrifice of your body, the Sacrifice of your time, and the Sacrifice of your resources. Religion in and of itself tends to grow flabby, soft, and indifferent when we do not give of ourselves beyond our comfort zone. The Christian who is saturated and bathed in the Christian spirit is willing to give "all" for the sake of the One who gave "all" for them.

Your church is called into a life of FAITHFUL service. The cause of Christ stands, loses, or fails through His disciples. Christ will not fail but the one doing the work can if distracted or not fully devoted to the cause can. Faithfulness requires diligence and determination. Fidelity is a virtue to be longed for. The definition of fidelity is faithfulness to a person, cause, or belief, demonstrated by continuing loyalty and support. It is not faithfulness as a result of itself, but faithfulness because of Christ. In the Amplified, *Rev. 2:10 says, "Fear nothing that you are about to suffer. Be aware that the devil is about to throw some of you into prison, that you may be tested [in your faith], and for ten days you will have tribulation. Be faithful to the point of death [if you must die for your faith], and I will give you the crown [consisting] of life."* Be faithful with your tithes, attendance, your service. Pay tithe even if you are not there. Go to services at church as much as possible. Help the cause of Christ in serving.

And finally, your church is called to a GLORIOUS service. We serve the Lord. The money we give in offerings and causes of the church is for the service and not for any return. It is not only the money but the time we serve is not to try to get something back in return but to give graciously and lovingly. Serving others at the park or giving a kind word is service giving glory to God and not us. *Matthew 6:33-34 says, "But seek first the kingdom of God and His righteousness, and all these things shall be added to you. Therefore, do not worry about tomorrow, for tomorrow will worry about its things. Sufficient for the day is its trouble."*

I hope that small church pastors, leaders, and members will stop wasting valuable energy trying to imitate large church ministry, and instead recognize the inherent and strategic strengths of small churches. That means getting excited about what God is doing and plans to do through your church. A small church with David's heart is one that has become comfortable being small. Because it has learned to recognize the unique advantages of its size. A small church with David's heart realizes it can accomplish things that larger churches cannot. It can proceed in ministry, not from a sense of its deficiencies, but confidence in its strengths.

"And whatever you do, do it heartily, as to the Lord and not to men, knowing that from the Lord you will receive the reward of the inheritance; for you serve the Lord Christ." (Colossians 3:23-24)

Telling our Story

The one thing that God has proven to me over and over at the small church that I pastor is that He is always faithful in rewarding His children when we are faithful in His call to us. Our church when it comes to numbers, facilities, finances, or volunteers, often feels as if we run dry. And when we rely on our abilities and our strength, we do run dry, but God springs up streams in the desert and provides plenty in the dry places. It has never ceased to amaze me how His blessings continue to flow upon us regardless of how desperate things may seem.

When we as a church were looking for opportunities to serve in our community, I went and talked to the school resource people at our schools in the town. In my discussion with them about how we could be partners with them, they gave me some ideas. They gave me a list of things to do to help the kids and we picked a small, seemingly insignificant thing to start doing to speak encouragement and love into kids' lives that are struggling and are at risk.

A piece of paper and a pen can make a difference in kids' lives. Don't underestimate the effect and power that God can demonstrate in lives – theirs and yours. One of the suggestions that were given was starting a pen Pal exchange with some of the more at-risk kids with some of the older adults in our church that could not get out and do much because of physical limitations. The pen pal notes – impacting small lives in a big way. Turned out to be good for the kids and the church members. The kids wrote wonderful little notes that kids do with questions that would make you chuckle, and the adults would in return answer questions back. The most wonderful thing about these notes was the words of encouragement that would be given to the kids to keep studying hard and pay attention in class so that they could be smart and productive someday in the world that they were growing up in. It was a treat for both sides when they received notes from each other. "Little is much when God is in it"

We have seen the need in our community, and we have responded with a little box on a stick in our parking lot. It started with one box where people could donate food or other needs in the box as they could give to others. Then people that had the need could come and take it from the box. Compared to the whole need for food insecurity it seems insignificant or even trivial. I even thought, how is this going to make any kind of difference? But God has placed His blessing on the effort, and it is multiplying over and over. At last count, there were at least 45 throughout our county and untold amounts of food have been provided and donated through those boxes. The love of God is being demonstrated through us using a little box. The shepherd's pantry – reaching people's physical and spiritual needs. "Little is much when God is in it."

Another small but effective ministry is the baby bottle campaign that raises money for an abortion alternative center in our neighborhood. The money for the baby bottles is for the good work of the center, helping to save the lives of babies and helping to prevent avoidable regret and guilt and shame of mothers.

We have a high school only one block from our church and we partner with the resource coordinator there and various things because they have about 50-60 students a year that are homeless. We help in many things but one thing that God showed Himself off was a fundraiser we did for the homeless student's caps and gowns. I was told that 13 students need caps and gowns for graduation and did not have the money to get them, so I started a social media fundraiser to raise the $650 needed for them. Within the first 3 hours, the funds were raised, and they kept coming in. 12 hours later $1500 was raised, and when 24 hours had passed, we had raised $6500. We were not only able to buy the caps and gowns, but the students also got to go on a senior trip to Florida with the resource coordinator and other staff. God is so good. "Littler is much when God is in it."

You do not have to be a big church with huge budgets, or a large staff to make a huge impact in your community and your church. As one wise man observed, "I place no hope in my strength, nor in my works; but all my confidence is in God my protector, who never abandons those who have put all their hope and thought in Him." Francois Rabelais. If we hold on to God… to His wisdom and His power… then we will succeed in this coming year. And we will lay hold of everything God wants us to have. Granted, it may seem to be that it may seem that our future may be in doubt at times… but the result will never really be in question.

In our culture, everything is defined by numbers. How much money you have in the bank account, how many people are sitting in the pews, and how many likes your church receives on Facebook determines your importance and what level of acceptance you receive among peers. If this is the only lens that we choose to look at ourselves as churches, then many would not measure up. Society seems to endorse the concept that "Bigger is better." Churches with fewer people, finances, and social media presence would feel inadequate and possibly second-class if this was the only measuring stick used to determine your church's effectiveness.

Thankfully God's economy runs on a whole different level. On a Heavenly level with a Heavenly perspective. God does not see small as a deficiency in the church, but as a great opportunity to do His great work through them. Larger congregations have their place and purpose, but the smaller churches cover more geographical areas and reach more population than anyone large church can do. Every church is important in the Kingdom of God. Every congregation is vital to the work of the Kingdom as a body of believers.

God is known for His use of small things to do great deeds throughout history. He uses a shepherd boy to unite and rule a small nation of Jewish people. God tells Gideon to take a small group of warriors to defeat an army of thousands. Jesus took a boy's small lunch and fed a multitude till they were full. Yet today, God takes individuals and small groups, and revival spring up for a great move down through the centuries.

Small churches have an even greater impact on the local community in which they are planted. Small churches are extremely important in our neighborhoods and towns across the nation. They are woven into the fabric of who the community is and are just as important to the people that live around them. The Kingdom work that small and rural churches do cannot be replaced. Because of the intimacy that they offer, small churches can speak the language of the local context. They can feel the pulse of the neighborhood that few could hope to imitate.

Every church regardless of the size, shape, or locality is vital to the work in the Kingdom. Every church is a part of the bigger body. Each church has a function in the body, whether they are an arm or a leg, or a toe or an eye. The small church can demonstrate the big heart, and big character, because we serve a big God that is building His big Kingdom. The small church needs to function with the confidence as one with great faith and a mustard seed..." I have a mustard seed and I'm not afraid to use it."

If we allow ourselves to surrender to God with total abandonment, He can take the smoldering ember that is struggling to survive in our churches, and He will cause the Holy Spirit to blow a wind of renewal over us in such a way that the revival fire can't help but to flare up in us. God wants His church to burn with passion within them in a way that every one that is around can't help but to feel the warmth and see the glow that is on us. God is represented by fire and we need to let our light so shine that the world can see Him in us.

"How beautiful on the mountains are the feet of those who bring good news, who proclaim peace, who bring good tidings, who proclaim salvation, who say to Zion, "Your God reigns!" Isaiah 52:7

"The fire must be kept burning on the altar continuously; it must not go out." (Leviticus 6:13)

Reflection Questions

1. How is it that God can use your church for His mighty works in your neighborhood?
2. Do you have the courage that was in David, Gideon, or the widow ladies to step out for God with confidence that He will be with you?
3. What small thing can God be calling you into today?

Best Practices/Ideas

1. Go to your local schools and meet with the administrators or resource people and see where they can suggest you get involved.
2. Be generous in some way to the needy in your community by giving out food, doing a cookout, or having a community dinner in your fellowship hall once a month.
3. Listen to what people around you say is the greatest need and see if there is anything you can do. Does not matter what, just do something.

NOTES

Chapter 1

1   Got Questions. Why was the fire in the altar to burn continuously (Leviticus 6:13)? https://www.gotquestions.org/altar-fire.html

Chapter 2

1   Dr. David F. Nixon, Oklahoma City, Dust Jacket Press, 2011. Walking the Leadership Higher Ground, 6

2   Dr. David F. Nixon, Oklahoma City, Dust Jacket Press, 2011. Walking the Leadership Higher Ground, 16

3   Mark A. Copeland, Executable Outlines, 2022. https://executableoutlines.com/textual_sermons/exo3_1.html

Chapter 3

1   Mark Steinmetz, *IMS Technology Services*, PERCEPTION VS. REALITY, Article. https://www.imsts.com/perception-vs-reality#

2   Allen Carr, The Sermon Notebook. http://www.sermonnotebook.org/old%20testament/Jer%206_16.htm

3   Mike Walls. The Old Paths. https://baptistresources.us/sermons-2/the-old-paths/

4   Robert Ringer, Reality VS Your Perception of Reality. https://www.earlytorise.com/truth-about-reality/

Chapter 4

1   Glenn Daman, Chicago, IL. Moody Publishers, 2018. The Forgotten Church, 15-16

2   Karl Vaters, If Small Churches Are Essential, Why Are We Not Fulfilling Our Potential?,January 24, 2022, Blog

Chapter 5

1   Got Questions, What is Prayer? https://www.gotquestions.org/what-is-prayer.html

2   Yvonne I. Wilson, Reclaim Your Identity And Regain Your Destiny, https://empowermentmomentsblog.com/2012/11/17/reclaim-your-identity-and-regain-your-destiny/. Posted on November 17, 2012

3   Charles E. Lawless Jr., Grand Rapids, MI. Zondervan. 2003. Serving in your church prayer ministry, 14-15

4   Charles E. Lawless Jr., Grand Rapids, MI. Zondervan. 2003. Serving in your church prayer ministry, 16

5   Charles E. Lawless Jr., Grand Rapids, MI. Zondervan. 2003. Serving in your church prayer ministry, 18

6   Charles E. Lawless Jr., Grand Rapids, MI. Zondervan. 2003. Serving in your church prayer ministry, 19

Chapter 6

1   Rick Rusaw and Eric Swanson, Loveland, CO. Group, 2004. The Externally Focused Church. 146

2   Rick Rusaw and Eric Swanson, Loveland, CO. Group, 2004. The Externally Focused Church. 150

3   Zig Ziglar, Carol Stream, IL. Tyndale House Publishers, 2009. Daily Insights with Zig Ziglar. Write it down! January 2.

4   Dr. Susan K. Smith, Walk through open doors, http://kineticslive.com/2017/08/22/walking-open-doors-tuesdaymeditation/

Chapter 7

Chapter 8

1   Thomasson, George A.,Orlando, FL. 2018.Renovate Publishing Group. Resuscitate: How to breathe new life into a gasping church. 58-59

2   Tiffany Deluccia, The Unstuck Church Group, What Strategic Planning Should Do for a Church, Jan. 10, 2022

3   Tony Morgan, Nashville, TN. Thomas Nelson, 2017. The Unstuck Church: equipping churches to experience sustained health. 65

Chapter 9

1   Bill Henard, How to Create Buy-In for Church Revitalization, Buy-in is the beginning point for revitalization, and buy-in is the ending point, June 11, 2018.

2   Tony Morgan, Nashville, TN. Thomas Nelson, 2017. The Unstuck Church: equipping churches to experience sustained health. 31-34

3   Michael Keller, 3 TRUTHS ABOUT GOD THAT FUEL GENEROSITY, OCTOBER 11, 2018, Blog

Chapter 10

1   Ed Stetzer and Philip Nation, Birmingham, AL. New Hope Publishers, 2008. Compelled By Love: The Most Excellent Way to Missional Living, 84-85

2   Ed Stetzer and Philip Nation, Birmingham, AL. New Hope Publishers, 2008. Compelled By Love: The Most Excellent Way to Missional Living, 100

3   Tim Cheser and Steve Timmus, Wheaton, IL. Crossway, 2012. Everyday Church: Gospel Communities on Mission, 111

4   Michael Frost, Colorado Springs, CO. Nav Press, 2016. Surprise the World: The Five Habits of Highly Missional People. 1

Chapter 11

1   Maggie Wooll, The importance of listening as a leader in the digital era, article for Better up. https://www.betterup.com/blog/the-importance-of-listening-as-a-leader-in-the-digital-era

2   Chris Colvin, July 19, 2018, Taking Risks in Ministry. https://influencemagazine.com/en/Practice/Taking-Risks-in-Ministry

3   Mark A. Copeland, The Greatest Need, Executable Outlines, 2022

Chapter 12

1   Sermon Central. https://www.sermoncentral.com/sermons/core-values-excellence-robert-simmons-sermon-on-character-90982

2   Christianity.com, https://www.christianity.com/church/church-history/timeline/1701-1800/henry-martyn-forsook-all-for-christ-11630337.html.

More Resources

The Revitalization Network can be found at:

https://www.ruralrevitalization.net/

You will be able to find resources and materials to help assist the pastor and church leaders to better navigate revitalization for their church and community.

Request to Join Our Private Facebook Page
The Revitalization Network

To be placed on our E-mail list go to
rural.revitalization.ky@gmail.com

Coming in 2023

Robert Beckett's next book to release:

God's Pattern for Revitalization
Restoring the Order and Purpose to God's Church

God's pattern for revitalization is remembering where you have drifted from. It's turning back to obedience and being radical disciples of Jesus Christ. It's not being content in your little Christian world, but it's going out into your community and being the light of Christ that can change hearts and lives, recognizing that we need to consecrate ourselves over again, humbling ourselves, seeking forgiveness, and pleading with God to bring revival to our nation once again. It's repenting of the waywardness of our relationship with Him, responding in such a way that turns our hearts and affections to God, finally returning to the place that we once occupied as God's people and church. We can do this! We *must* do this! The time is now. Will you answer the call?

Coming 2023-2024

On-line Video Course

"Revive Us!"
Revitalizing Your Church for Revival

Narrated and instructed by Robert Beckett

Is your church on the verge of, or experiencing decline or stagnation?
Has your church been experiencing this for quite some time? If you
have not seen any new visitors, new families, conversions, or baptisms
for what seems like forever, then your church has plateaued or is in
a serious decline. If you are a pastor who is attempting to revitalize
a dying, struggling, or stagnating church, this course is for you.

The "Revive Us" video course is a five-module journey that
will inspire and equip you to revitalize your church. I will walk
you through this course to help you to navigate revitalization
for your church. I am a pastor that knows the struggles of
revitalization firsthand. You will be given the tools you need
to implement a revitalization plan in your own church.

In this course, you will learn insight and answer questions like:

-Is revitalization right for my church?
-What does it take to revive a church?
-How will we implement a revitalization plan?
-What are the challenges and obstacles of church revitalization?
-And much more!